TUDOR WARSHIP **MARY ROSE**

TUDOR WARSHIP
MARY ROSE

Douglas McElvogue

Naval Institute Press
Annapolis, Maryland

ANATOMY OF THE SHIP

ALSO AVAILABLE

THE 100-GUN SHIP VICTORY
ISBN 978–1–8448–6223–8

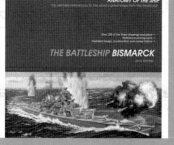

THE BATTLESHIP BISMARCK
ISBN 978–1–8448–6224–5

THE USS CONSTITUTION
ISBN 978–1–5911–4250–8

This highly acclaimed series aims to provide the finest documentation of individual ships and ship types ever published. It is a radical departure from the usual monograph approach, which concentrates on either the ship's service history, its technical details or external appearance. All of these aspects are included in the 'Anatomy of the Ship', but what makes the series unique is a complete set of line drawings, both the conventional type of plan as well as explanatory perspective views. Although elaborate drawings are extremely popular in aviation publications, this is the first attempt to document ships in similar depth — literally down to the nuts and bolts.

These drawings are accurate, visually exciting and totally comprehensive, offering ship buffs, historians and model makers a novel insight into the technicalities of each ship type covered.

THE AUTHOR

Douglas McElvogue was Senior Research Fellow and Archaeologist at the Mary Rose Trust and specialises in maritime archaeological reconstructions.

Conway
An imprint of Bloomsbury Publishing Plc

50 Bedford Square
London
WC1B 3DP
UK
www.bloomsbury.com

1385 Broadway
New York
NY 10018
USA

CONWAY™ is a trademark and imprint of Bloomsbury Publishing Plc

First published 2015
© Douglas McElvogue, 2015

Douglas McElvogue has asserted his right under the Copyright, Designs and Patents Act, 1988, to be identified as Author of this work.

Published and distributed in the United States of America and Canada by the Naval Institute Press, 291 Wood Road, Annapolis, Maryland 21402-5043
www.nip.org

British Library Cataloguing-in-Publication Data
A catalogue record for this book is available from the British Library.

LOC number 2015942053

ISBN 978 1 59114 181 5

2 4 6 8 10 9 7 5 3 1

Designed by CE Marketing
Printed and bound in China by RRD South China

Bloomsbury Publishing Plc makes every effort to ensure that the papers used in the manufacture of our books are natural, recyclable products made from wood grown in well-managed forests. Our manufacturing processes conform to the environmental regulations of the country of origin.

To find out more about our authors and books visit www.bloomsbury.com. Here you will find extracts, author interviews, details of forthcoming events and the option to sign up for our newsletters.

CONTENTS

PREFACE

The process of research and reconstruction is often a learning process in its own right. Solutions to problems go through a number of iterations and refinements, as more is learned or discarded as we start to understand more of what we are studying. My work on the *Mary Rose* is no different, and this book has served to formulate and reassess thoughts and ideas concerning the *Mary Rose* and her build. However, a line has to be drawn and something produced. I have drawn that line at a stage where the overall generic concepts could be presented. It is now only the finer detail that needs to be worked on and this requires years of work in the archives where eventually I am sure we will find a truth if not the whole truth.

Background

This book is based on work carried out by the author at the Mary Rose Trust (the Trust or MRT) between April 2002 and November 2006, and subsequent research afterwards. During that time I was employed as Senior Research Fellow and Archaeologist for the Mary Rose Trust with a remit to record (physically within the ship hall) and research the ship, its construction and its associated fastenings and fittings. As part of this remit I would often find myself in the museum recording the remains of the ship and its artefacts. It was during one of these visits that I overheard members of the public discussing the Mary Rose Trust's official reconstruction of the *Mary Rose*, displayed as a model. The gist of their conversation was that it looked nothing like the *Mary Rose*. They expected to see something different,

Fig 1 Anthony Roll illustration of the *Mary Rose*.

The Anthony Roll

The Anthony Roll is a list of Henry VIII's navy, presented to him at the end of his reign in 1546. Originally compiled by Anthony Anthony (a clerk in the ordnance office) before and after the *Mary Rose* sank, it is the only known named representation of the ship. It is a list of all 58 ships of the King's navy, starting with the great ship *Henry Grace à Dieu* and ending with the smallest row barges.

Each vessel entry consists of a painting of the named vessel accompanied by its size, number of crew, details of their guns, shot small firearms, longbows, arrows, pikes, and bills and related equipment, called habiliments of war.

Painted onto long vellum sheets, the original 'rolls' of vellum were kept in the Royal Library until separated by Charles II. Two rolls, which included the painting of the *Mary Rose*, were given to the famous diarist Samuel Pepys. The third remained in royal hands until sold to the British Library. Pepys, who was compiling early documents for his history of the navy, had his rolls cut up and bound into a single volume. This volume can still be seen today in the Pepys Library at Magdalene College, Cambridge.

something more akin to the iconic Anthony Roll illustration of the ship (Fig 1). As I carried out my research, with an open but inquisitive mind, I found myself asking more questions of the archaeology than I was getting answers. This especially concerned the shape and size of the bow and forecastle as well as the summercastle. Within a year I became more inclined to agree with the public perception of the ship (McElvogue 2003).

Intention

The official reconstruction of the *Mary Rose* was designed by Andrew Fielding as part of the Bassett-Lowke model project (Fielding) and replicated by the Trust until 2003 (Fig 2). This reconstruction represents an Elizabethan-style galleon and not a great ship of Henry VIII's navy. Fielding's *Mary Rose* is best presented as the minimalist reconstruction, based purely on the remaining archaeology (Fig 3) without any further extrapolation ie no more decks than allowed for by the physical remains of the ship as found. For this reason the bow, with its galleon-style forecastle, was designed around the low level of the sterncastle.

This reconstruction, however, does not fit with what we now know about the *Mary Rose*; not only from her archaeology (Marsden 2009) but also from documents (Spont; Knighton and Loades 2000 and 2002) and the single named picture of her. As such the Trust has refined its reconstruction to include an extra deck in the stern and a larger overhanging forecastle

Fig 2 Model of the *Mary Rose* based on the Bassett-Lowke model.

(Marsden 2009, p370–379). However, this outlined shape does not agree with that of the latest image of the ship as painted by Geoff Hunt (see front jacket flap of this book). While a good representation of the *Mary Rose,* the forecastle and details of it do not tally with the Anthony Roll illustration or the known archaeology of the ship and its documentation. Furthermore, Marsden suggests that different reconstructions can be given for the *Mary Rose*. This might be true for the interpretation of the decks; however, this is not the case for the hull. The original hull form can, without doubt, be reconstructed with 100 per cent certainty.

It is therefore the intention within this anatomy of the *Mary Rose* to reconcile as much as is reasonably possible of the archaeology of the ship with the Anthony Roll illustration in combination with historical documentation (Fig 4). The archaeology now includes the recently found and recorded stempost, which allows for an authoritative reconstruction of the hull, as well as features and artefacts recovered during the recent excavations (2003–2006) not published by the Trust in their publications. The documentation includes never seen or used

before contemporary descriptions of the ship and parts of her. For those of an archaeological or theoretical bent, this can be classed as a full and maximal (literally) reconstruction.

Decks

Admittedly the one area of contention will be three decks in the summercastle. This is based on a maximal interpretation of the Anthony Roll's stern using all the deck terms found in the archives (Fig 5). This is two more decks than the minimalist reconstruction has; it having only the summercastle. The compromise between the two reconstructions is a *Mary Rose* with two decks fore and aft and not three (Fig 6). This is probably the *Mary Rose* that people can accept as it is not as lofty as three decks. An alternative to this arrangement is for the forecastle to be left as three decks (Fig 7). As far as the anatomy of the *Mary Rose* is concerned, the differences in the deck arrangements do not matter as all the information for the maximum reconstruction is given. If the modeller or other interested person wishes to change the arrangement of the decks, only those decks wanted need be included.

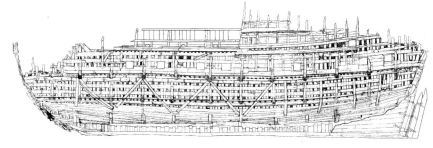

Fig 3 The archaeological remains of the *Mary Rose* as recorded in the ship hall (not to scale – see also page 136).

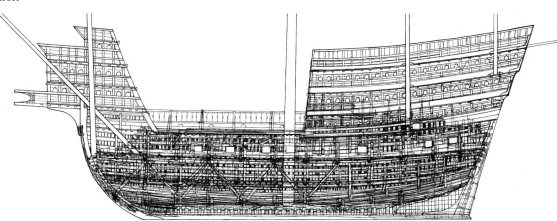

Fig 4 The archaeological remains of the *Mary Rose* superimposed over the Anthony Roll reconstruction of the ship (not to scale – see also page 136).

Fig 5 The Anthony Roll's interpretation of deck terms found in the archives. The principal areas of the ship are identified here:

1 Poop 2 Deck above the summercastle 3 Summercastle 4 Nether deck 5 Orlop or lower orlop 6 Breast of summercastle 7 Pavise waist 8 Cubbridge head 9 Barbican 10 Forecastle 11 Upper forecastle 12 Highest deck.

Scope

While based on the archaeology of the *Mary Rose* (her physical remains, iconography and historical documentation), this is not an archaeological or research publication. Therefore the detailed research, interpretation and design-making process is not described or presented here in full; only the conclusions are given. For an archaeological description of the ship, the Mary Rose Trust archaeological reports should be consulted while the numerous popular publications by Alexander McKee, Margaret Rule, Bradford, and more recently Knighton and Loades as well as David Childs, give more than enough information on the general background and history of the ship and its rediscovery, excavation and recovery. Only a cursory description is given here. Those interested in a more detailed description of the reconstruction process, as well as interpreting and defining the original hull form and design concept, should consult McElvogue's *The Stem post. Defining the bows and hull shape of the Marye Rosse* and *Riddle in the Rose;* while the sailing capabilities of the ship are analysed in McElvogue's '…the best trial that could be…'

References

Bradford, E, *The Story of the Mary Rose*, Hamish Hamilton, 1982

Childs, D, *The Warship Mary Rose: The Life & Times of King Henry VIII's Flagship,* Chatham Publishing, 2007

Fielding, A, 'The Mary Rose – a Model', unpublished monograph, Mary Rose Trust, 1995

Knighton, CS and Loades, DM (Eds), *The Anthony Roll of Henry VIII's Navy*, Navy Records Society/Ashgate, 2000

Knighton, CS and Loades, DM, *Letters from the Mary Rose*, Sutton, 2002

Marsden, P (Ed), *The 'Mary Rose': Your Noblest Shippe: Anatomy of a Tudor Warship*, Archaeology of the 'Mary Rose' Vol II, Mary Rose Trust, 2009

McElvogue, DM, *The Mary Rose - what did she look like? A consideration of contemporary iconography and current archaeology*, unpublished lecture notes and PowerPoint, Mary Rose Trust, 2003

McElvogue, DM, *Riddle in the Rose*, unpublished lecture notes and PowerPoint, Mary Rose Trust, 2006

McElvogue, DM, '…the best trial that could be…', unpublished lecture notes and PowerPoint, Mary Rose Trust, 2007a

McElvogue, DM, *The Stem post. Defining the bows and hull shape of the Marye Rosse*, unpublished lecture notes and PowerPoint, Mary Rose Trust, 2007b

McKee, A, *King Henry VIII's Mary Rose*, Souvenir Press, 1973

Rule, M, *The Mary Rose*, Conway Maritime Press, 1982

Rule, M, *The Mary Rose, The Excavation and Raising of Henry VIII's Flagship*, Conway Maritime Press, 1983 Second Edition, 1986

Rule, M, *The Mary Rose: a guide*, Mary Rose Trust, 1986

Spont, A (Ed), Letters and papers relating to the War with France, 1512–1513, Navy Records Society, Vol 10, 1897

Fig 6 *Mary Rose* with two decks fore and aft (A) Internal (B) External (not to scale – see also page 70).

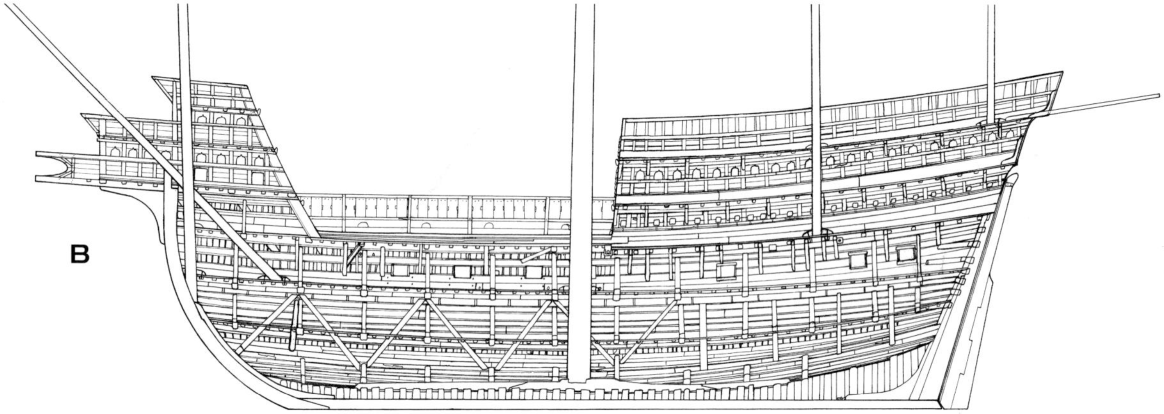

Principal hull dimensions

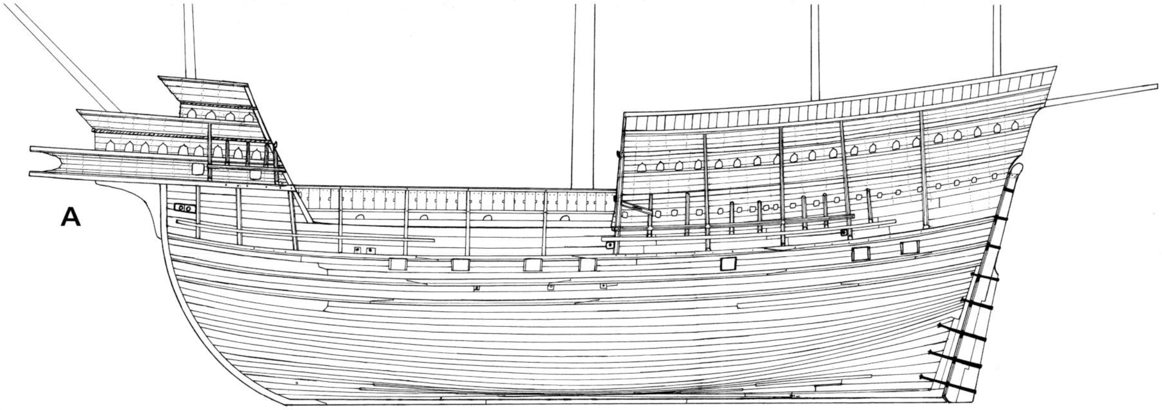

	Imperial	Metric
Keel length o/a	101ft 8 $^{15}/_{32}$ in	31m
Waterline length	125ft 3 $^{30}/_{32}$ in	38.2m
Hull length o/a (between perpendiculars)	131ft 2 $^{26}/_{32}$ in	40m
Maximum length o/a	163ft 2 $^{21}/_{32}$ in	49.7m
Maximum breadth outside plank to outside plank	38ft 3in	11.7m
Depth of hold ceiling planking to underside of orlop deck plank	13ft 5 $^{21}/_{32}$ in	4.1m
Draught amidships	17ft 8 $^{19}/_{32}$ in	5.4m
Draught forwards	17ft $^{19}/_{32}$ in	5.2m
Draught aft	18ft $^{17}/_{32}$ in	5.5m
Tons and tonnage (keel length x breadth x depth of hold) ÷ 100	518 tons	

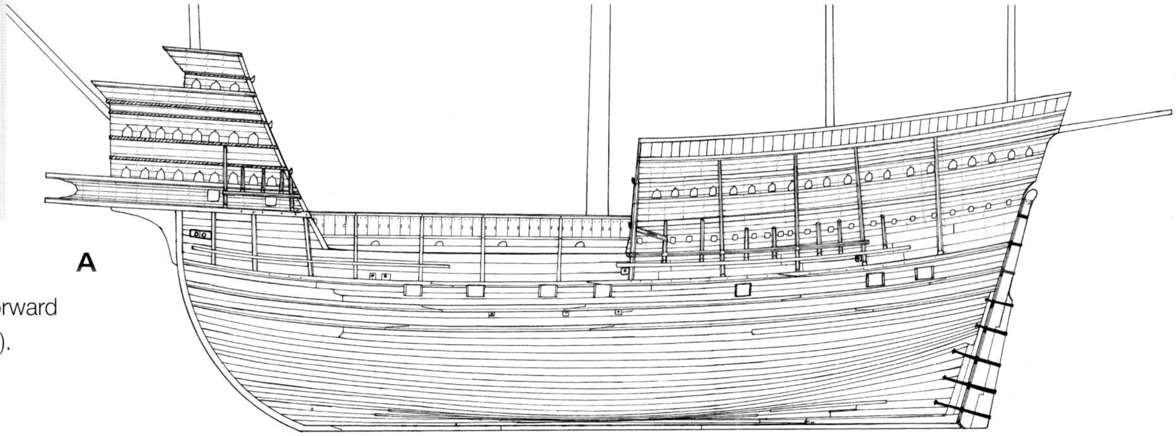

Fig 7 *Mary Rose* with two decks aft and three decks forward (A) External (B) Internal (not to scale – see also page 70).

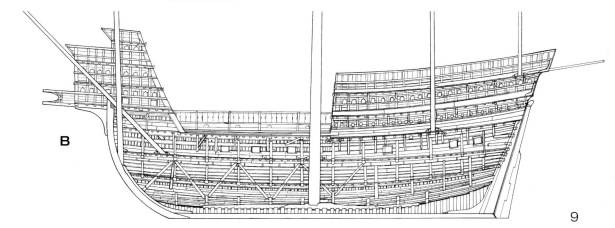

Introduction

The Tudor dynasty saw momentous changes in the political and religious structure of the British Isles. When Henry VII ascended the throne (1485) the British Isles were ruled by the two neighbouring kingdoms of England and Scotland as well as the Principality of Wales. The end of the Tudor dynasty, marked by the death of Elizabeth I (1603), saw the unification of the Scottish and English crown. Wales had already been amalgamated with England when Cromwell instigated his great statute for the resumptions of all franchises and liberties of the crown in 1536 (Loades 1986, p175). The reign of the Tudors also saw a change in political power, with the erosion of the old aristocracies and a rise of parliamentary power. Furthermore the break with Rome and the Catholic faith increased the power of the monarchy and hailed the arrival of the Protestant faith in England.

Henry VIII, the most potent of England's renaissance monarchs, acceded to the throne on 21 April 1509, at the tender age of 17 (Fig 8). By the end of the year, Henry had started to spend his wealth on two new Great Ships, the *Mary Rose* and *Peter Pomegranate*. Both ships were completed in the summer of 1511 and saw their first service in the French War of 1512. The *Mary Rose* had a long and honourable career spanning the whole of Henry's reign, being launched within three years of his accession, and was cast away two years before he died. During this time Henry had changed the political, social and religious horizons of the nation.

Political background to Henry VIII's accession

Henry Tudor (Henry VII) came to the throne in a period of considerable unrest when the powers of the Crown had been eroded, but more importantly a time when the resources of the Crown had been depleted. By centralising government through devices such as the Commission of the Peace and the Councils of the Marches of Wales and the North, Henry increased his ability to draw upon the resources of his subjects (Loades 1986, p114–127). Large scale and co-ordinated rebellion or protest, such as the Pilgrimage of Grace, could still happen but they became fewer and further between. Despite his increasing power, Henry had

Fig 8 Young Henry VIII.

to have Parliament's consent to raise extra revenue. But ever resourceful, he sidestepped Parliament to use traditional county levies to recruit an army for France without opposition (Loades 1986). With such careful manipulation of his traditional political powers, Henry raised the authority of the Crown, added weight to its patronage and conversely increased the exposure of royal authority. Royal regulation and patronage permeated down through English society via Henry's statutes and proclamations, from the great noble families through to the lower classes. The ports, merchants and sailors of England were not to be left alone.

Against this background, Henry VII increased the bureaucratic powers of the Council for Marine Causes. The council had officers in Deptford, Woolwich and Portsmouth. Henry increased its network of victuallers and suppliers of ship making material as well as the 'ordinary' budget for such supplies. Although the King was the final arbitrator and creditor, he still relied heavily on the services and support of his subjects (Davies, p268–286), and in doing so he courted their support. In the Navigational Acts of 1486 and 1489, Henry VII confined the increasingly lucrative Gascon wine trade to 'English bottoms', or sold special licences to Spanish merchants to carry the trade to Bristol, creating an additional source of income (Loades 2000, p28). At the same time Henry VII supported Cabot's voyages across the Atlantic and his Bristol subjects opened up the cod fisheries of the Newfoundland Banks (Fig 9). By the 1520s the fishing fleet numbered scores of ocean-going ships; despite being a good training ground for the navy, neither Henry VII nor Henry VIII offered it financial support.

When Henry VII came to the throne, entrepreneurial English merchants were already trading off the Azores and during his reign expanded into Madeira. Despite this, the increasing Tudor bureaucracy was used to increase the revenue and control of the Crown, not to fund overseas expansion and explorations or the sciences. Initially Henry VIII followed suit, though by the end of his reign he had come to appreciate that the new sciences should be supported and could be put to royal uses.

The newfound stability was not nurtured solely through political means. Henry VII created a large siege train, which rendered meaningless acts of defiance by a noble's military strength. Henry's new powers and greater resources invested in the Crown meant that few individuals could consider waging a private war against the Crown. Gone were the days where the most powerful subjects could afford to wage a private war (as had happened in the War of the Roses). To crown his achievements, Henry built two 'Great Ships' the *Sovereign* and the *Regent*.

Fig 9 The replica of Cabot's *Mathew*.

Fig 10 The remains of the *Henry Grace à Dieu* on the Hamble.

The English shipbuilding tradition

Ships in the Medieval period were known by the terms keel, cog and hulk. The keel was a clinker-built vessel epitomised by the Viking longship and knar, the cog its Germanic equivalent, which incorporated clinker sides with a carvel bottom, and the enigmatic hulk (only seen on seals) was a clinker-built ship of some form. The predominant keel of the 10th to 12th centuries was superseded by the cog in the 12th to 14th centuries only to be reinstated in the 15th and 16th centuries as a larger, more extreme version with triple clinker, as seen by the remains of Henry V's *Henry Grace à Dieu* on the River Hamble (Fig 10). In this extreme form, clinker construction had reached the end of its development. This nomenclature referred to construction (hence the reason for seeking a different form of construction for the hulk) in a time when, as a general rule, ships and boats in northern Europe only had one mast and one sail. During the 15th century this was to change as Henry V introduced two-masted carracks from southern regions, which resulted in the three-masted but still clinker-built *Henry Grace à Dieu*.

Henry VII inherited eight ships when he won the English crown on the battle field at Bosworth. Although considered a frugal king, Henry knew any monarch who wished to be considered on the European political stage had to have ships of prestige. All the main European powers had a maritime arm as the hard end of diplomacy. Henry built two Great Ships, the *Regent* (600 tons) and the *Sovereign* (450 tons), both of which were built in carvel fashion and, apart from the all important transom stern and ports with port lids, were the precursors of the *Mary Rose*. When Henry VIII ascended the throne he followed his father's lead and ordered his new ships to be built in carvel fashion.

English carvel shipbuilding

Henry VII was not the first monarch to construct a carvel royal ship, this claim belongs to his Yorkist predecessor Edward IV. Edward, whose untimely death eventually resulted in the Tudor dynasty, built the *Edward* at Dunwich in 1464 (Loades 2000, p14). Later he offered a reward to Bristol shipwrights to construct a carvel ship on the Portuguese model, encouraged an expansion of maritime trade, petitioned the Pope to such an effect and settled foreign craftsmen in England so they could pass on their skills

(Loades 2000, p18). Despite this, and more probably due to the unrest caused by Edward's death, at the time of Henry VII's accession clinker-built ships still appear to be the dominant English form, though not for royal Great Ships.

From the beginning of Henry VIII's reign he embraced carvel construction and all the royal Great Ships would be carvel built. The reason for this appears to have been his passion for all things new that might show off his greatness. At sea this meant royal Great Ships built in the latest style and form, carrying the grandest but also deadliest weapons; the most potent ordnance the gun founders could cast.

Henry VIII built or purchased large carvel ships capable of carrying the latest and largest in cast bronze and wrought iron ordnance (Fig 11). To carry such large guns meant mounting them on a continuous deck low down and not just in the waist. It was the development of this continuous gun deck, enclosed from the worst of the weather, that was the conceptual revolution manifested for the first time in the *Mary Rose*. The guns therefore had to fire through the side of the ship through ports, which were now close to the waterline and therefore had to be lidded to stop them shipping water in rough weather. To maximise the number of heavy guns carried low down, a transom stern was built. This allowed the ship's designer to project the width of the main deck further aft and therefore allowed more guns to be carried aft in the ship and not just at its widest point in the waist.

Fig 12 *HMS Victory* with the Mary Rose Ship Hall behind, not too far from where the *Mary Rose* was built.

Early Portsmouth Dockyard

The dockyard at Portsmouth is on the eastern side of the harbour near the entrance. In 1495 King Henry VII appointed John Nest to Portsmouth to oversee the building of a new dock. He lasted three weeks until replaced by Robert Brigandine as Clerk of Ships and officer in charge of the construction of the dry dock at Portsmouth. The site is thought to be around the present No1 basin a few metres in front *HMS Victory* (Fig 12). The dock was designed by Sir Reginald Bray, the designer of St George's Chapel, Windsor, and Henry VII Chapel, Westminster Abbey. The work started in June 1495 and went on for 46 weeks, with never more than 60 men on site, until 29 November of the same year when it closed down for winter. On 25 February 1496 the gates were hung, which were the full width of the dock, spaced apart, the area in between filled with stones and clay rammed solid (Oppenheim, p143–158).

The first vessel docked was the *Sovereign* on 25 May 1496. It was docked with the aid of the crew and 140 other men taking a day and a night, and costing 24 shillings and 8 pence. All the men were fed on the job at a cost of 5 shillings and tuppence for bread, ten shillings for fish, and 13 shillings and 4 pence for ale. The *Sovereign* was in the dock for eight months,

Fig 11 Guns in the Mary Rose Museum.

which after refitting cost £595 6s 5d. In January c1497 work started on undocking the ship which cost £12 8s 2d; 10 times more than the docking costs (Oppenheim 1896a, p170). To help cover the costs, the *Sovereign* was chartered to a firm of merchants in Southampton for a trip to the Levant. For the first time in English naval history the dock gave Henry a permanent base to grave and work on a ship in the dry. After the *Sovereign,* the dock was enlarged to take the larger *Henry Grace à Dieu* and from then on it remained in service until c1623 when it was filled in. The *Mary Rose* was built in the dry dock and launched from there sometime in late spring, early summer of 1511, before being transported to the Thames for her final fitting

out. The *Mary Rose* would use the dry dock at times of need as noted in November 1514 (RNM, MSS, 08).

Building the *Mary Rose*

The first possible indirect reference to the building of the *Mary Rose* is a private Venetian letter from England dated 30 December 1509. This letter refers to a marked increase in the price of tin caused by the King buying a great quantity to make 100 pieces of artillery. The letter also states Henry wished to launch and arm four ships, which he had been building in Hampton (ie Southampton). Unfortunately neither the ship's names nor their tonnage is given (CSP I–I 287, p133), nor is it made clear that the artillery is for them. However, knowing that the *Regent, Sovereign, Mary Rose* and *Peter Pomegranate* were all being worked on at this time (though their names may be unknown), and paid for by the '…customers … of the Port of Southampton…' (Knighton and Loades 2002, p8), it is not unreasonable to assume the ships were being built in Southampton as opposed to Portsmouth.

The principal vessels of Henry's fleet

Name	Built	Tons	Fate
Henry Grace à Dieu	1514	1500	Renamed *Edward* 1547, burned 1553
Peter Pomegranate	1510	450	Dropped 1558
Matthew	Bought 1545	600	Dropped 1554
Great Bark	1515	500/600	Rebuilt as *White Bear* 1564, sold 1629
Jesus of Lubeck	Hired 1544, bought 1545	600/700	Abandoned at San Juan d'Ulloa 1568
Pauncy (Pansy)	1543	450	Dropped 1557
Morian of Danzig	Bought 1545	500	Sold 1551
Struse of Danzig	Hired and bought 1544	400	Sold 1553
Mary Hamburg	Hired 1544, bought 1545	400	Sold 1555
Christopher of Bremen	Hired 1544 bought 1545	400/500	Sold 1555
Trinity Harry	Built 1530	250	Sold 1566
Small Bark	Built 1512	160	Dropped 1553
Sweepstake	Built 1535	300	Dropped 1559
Minion	Built 1523	180	Dropped 1570
Lartique	French prize 1543	140	Sold 1547
Mary Thomas	French prize 1543	90	Dropped 1546
Hoy Bark		24	
George	1546	100	Still listed in 1588
Mary James	1543	60	1546

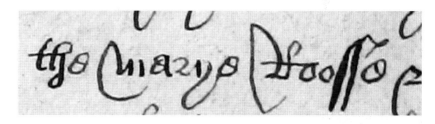

Fig 13 An early written reference to the *Mary Rose* being docked.

In the first six months of his reign, the young Henry had taken the decision to build the *Mary Rose* and *Peter Pomegranate* and refit the two Great Ships he inherited, the *Regent* and *Sovereign*. A month later (29 January 1510) Henry VIII initialled a warrant for workmanship not only on the *Regent* and *Sovereign* but also '…two new ships to be made for us, £700, and the one ship to be of the burden of 400 tons and the other ship to be of the burden of 300 tons…' (PRO E404/87/1 5944). The two new ships are the *Mary Rose* and *Peter Pomegranate*. This is confirmed the following year in an exchange of letters (dated 9 June 1511 and 30 June 1511) in response to money expended between Robert Brigandine (Clerk of the Ships) and Richard Palshide and John Dawtrey (Customs Officers, Southampton). In the original warrant for workmanship (29 January 1510), both the *Regent* and *Sovereign* are mentioned with the ships of 300 and 400 tons. In the following exchange of letters again the same four ships are referred to. In the earlier letter Brigandine wishes that

'…as well for the repairing of the *Sovereign* as [and] for the new making of the *Mary Rose* and *Peter Pomegranate* [to be invoiced] jointly together…' while the work done on the regent should be invoiced separately (Knighton and Loades 2002, p1). It is notable that the Clerk of Ships refers to all four ships by name (Fig 13) while Dawtrey and Palshide refer to the two older ships the *Regent* and *Sovereign* by name and the two new ships by tonnage.

Naming the *Mary Rose*

Every ship and boat from time immemorial has had a name and the *Mary Rose* was no different. Much has been made of the fact that Henry VIII's sister was called Mary and therefore the ship was named after her and the Tudor family emblem the Rose (Marsden 2003, p150). After all the *Great Galley* was also known as the *Princess Mary*, and also as the *Virgin Mary* (Anderson 1920, p274). Using his sister's name is seen as a sign of Henry's secular ideas and thoughts of personal grandeur. The fact that the largest ship was called the *Henry Grace à Dieu* (grace of God) is used as supporting evidence; however, this bears no resemblance to what we know of Henry VIII, nice as the story is. After all *Henry Grace à Dieu* means Henry in the grace of God, and was a term used by Henry's predecessors. Just like the *Henry Grace à Dieu* ships had also been named *Mary de Rose* before and after Henry's sister's birth and long after she had been forgotten. Edward IV knew of a ship of that name *Marrye de Rosse* (Quinn, p276), and 'Bloody Mary' the Catholic revisionist and daughter of Henry VIII named a newly built ship after its predecessor.

Fig 15 (left) Panelling with religious imagery. Fig 16 (right) A wooden rosary.

At his accession Henry was a devout Catholic, willing to defend the faith and go on pilgrimage to thank his lord for the blessing of a male heir. Therefore, there is no reason to believe that he would consider naming his revolutionary royal Great Ship after his sister, a secular pawn in the chess game of European politics. If it were the case then surely we would now have the *Princess Mary* and not the *Mary Rose*. Instead as a devout Catholic, Henry named his most revolutionary royal Great Ship after the most potent female in religious history, the mother of the son of God, otherwise known as the Virgin Mary, Saint Mary, Mary the mystic Rose or Mary de Rose translated as Mary the Rose, shortened to Mary Rose. Every Catholic in Christendom would recognise this symbolism.

The Virgin Mary is at the pinnacle of religious symbolism, second only by the Holy Trinity (God, Jesus son of God, and the Holy Ghost). The cult of the Virgin Mary had a strong following (including Henry's grandmother and father as well as himself), and is associated with the Rose (Starkey, p52 and p70). The Rose is a strong religious symbol, and is also a royal crest of the Tudor family (Fig 14). It may be used to represent the messianic promise, the nativity of Christ, and in this context the Virgin Mary (her rose is white for purity), or martyrdom (a red rose). There is no reason to doubt that the *Mary Rose* was named after the Virgin Mary, Saint Mary and her saint's symbol the rose, which also coincided with the crest of the Tudor family, the Tudor Rose. Naming his first ship after the Virgin Mary, however, had greater symbolic meaning to Henry than just devout religious symbolism, it also had military intent.

Fig 14 The Royal Crest on a bronze cannon recovered from the *Mary Rose*.

On his coronation Henry was anointed. The anointment used holy oils given to St Thomas Becket in a vision by the Virgin Mary. The Virgin Mary (Mary de Rose) told Becket that the oils were to be the unction of the Kings of England. Not the ones then on the throne but the '…Kings of the English…' who '…shall arise who will be anointed with this oil … the first to be anointed with this oil … shall recover by force the land lost by his forefathers, that is to say, Normandy and Aquitaine'. This became part of the legitimising of the Lancastrian then Tudor claim to the throne. But for Henry it was more than this (Starkey, p292). With the patronage of the Virgin Mary through her anointing oils, Henry legitimised his intentions for a forthcoming war with France. The naming of his first and revolutionary ship *Mary Rose* was therefore also a portent of his military intention towards the old enemy, France.

The *Mary Rose* was to represent the first flowering of the English Naval tradition; being the first in a line of purpose-built warships to fire a broadside of heavy guns on a continuous deck. Such ships were not expected to pay their way, unlike their forefathers and the contemporary converted merchantmen, such as *Jesus of Lubeck*. Thus the building of such ships saw the foundation of a permanent naval administration to oversee their building, arming and maintenance.

References
Calendar of State Papers (CSP) I–I, 287, p133
Public Records Office, now National Archives, Kew (PRO) E404/87/1 5944
Royal Naval Museum (RNM) MSS 8
Anderson, RC, *Henry VIII's 'Great Galley'*, The Mariner's Mirror, Vol 6, Issue 3, p274–81, 1920
Davies, CSL, *The Administration of the Royal Navy under Henry VIII*, English Historical Review, LXXX 268–86, 1965
Loades, DM, *Politics and the Nation, 1450–1660: Obedience, Resistance and Public Order*, Fontana Press, 1986
Loades, DM, *England's Maritime Empire: Seapower, Commerce and Policy, 1490–1690*, Longman, 2000
Marsden P, *Sealed By Time: The Loss and Recovery of the Mary Rose*, The Archaeology of the Mary Rose, Vol 1, Mary Rose Trust, 2003
Oppenheim, M (Ed), *Naval Accounts and Inventories of the reign of Henry VII, 1485–8 and 1495–7*, 1896a
Quinn, DB, 1935, *Edward IV and Exploration*, The Mariner's Mirror, Vol 21, Issue 3, p275–84, 1935
Starkey, D, *Henry: Virtuous Prince*, Harper Perennial, 2009

Fig 17 The inscription reads: 'SIT DEUS NOBIS CUN [sic] QUID CONTRA NOS' ('If God be for us who can be against us') around a rose and crown motif containing three feathers.

'...delivered and paid unto the said John Dawtrey ... for timber, ironworks, and workmanship of two new ships to be **made** for us £700...' (Knighton and Loades 2005, p5).

Building the *Mary Rose* was termed *'made'* by the Tudors, but before the ship could be built a number of decisions had to be made. First, an idea as to the ship's overall size was required, from which an understanding of the prerequisite resources in raw materials, manpower, area required for building the ship and the all-important financial resources for funding the enterprise could be discerned. Henry VIII decided to build the ship that was to become the *Mary Rose* as a 500-ton vessel. Once this had been decided it was easy for the master shipwright to decide on the three main dimensions of the ship; its keel length, maximum breadth and depth of hold. These three dimensions would help to shape the rest of the hull. It was at this stage that Henry appears to have made a brave and daring decision, to arm the larger of the two new ships with a primary armament of heavy ship killing guns. These would be mounted on a continuous and enclosed deck near the waterline where the gun ports would require lids to stop them from shipping water in heavy seas.

Design concept

(see drawings A1–A5 on page 23)
The hull of the *Mary Rose* was shaped by its English shipwrights to a preconceived design based around a number of traditional but rudimentary rules. The overall size of the ship would be decided upon, in this case a great ship of about 500 tons. From this the basic dimensions could be decided, these being: the length of keel (100ft), moulded breadth (38ft) and depth of hold from the top of the keel to the bottom of the orlop deck beam (13ft). For the *Mary Rose* this gives a tonnage measurement of 502 tons (100 x 38 x 13 ÷ 100) obviously rounded to 500 tons for the administrators (McElvogue 2006).

The second stage was to define the centre of the ship, where its broadest section would be and conversely where the master frame would be set up (A1). From here the distance to where the quarter frames would be raised and the division of the ship could be worked out. This was done by using a simple formula of ratios, dividing the length of the keel by three then dividing the middle section by five, the second foremost sector thus being the centre of the ship (A2) (McElvogue 2007b).

The third stage is to design the master and quarter moulds (A3), as well as define the arc of the stempost and rake of the sternpost. The master mould was defined by a large arc projecting off a small flat with deadrise from the

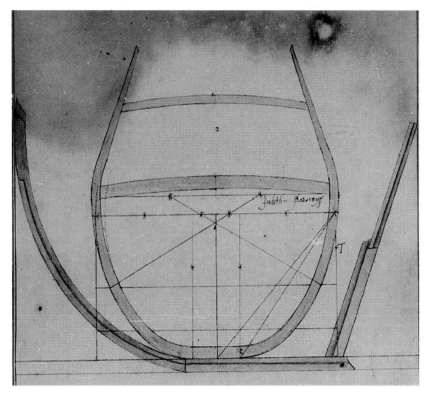

Fig 18 The basic design concept as presented from *Fragments of Ancient Shipwrightry* by Mathew Baker.

keel through the bilge and up to the orlop deck where a second arc defined the upper curvature of the hull. The quarter moulds are defined in the same way but have the cord of their arc shorted, while at the same time the centre point pulled in (A4) and raised (A5). In this way the shape of the hull could be defined and controlled (Fig 18). Once the main shape of the *Mary Rose* was defined, the form of construction had to be decided. Henry chose to build the *Mary Rose* using carvel technique, incorporating three revolutionary features, a full gun deck, lidded gunports and a transom stern.

Clinker or carvel planking

The English were familiar with carvel-built ships, the first being noted in English documents between 1463 and 1466 (Friel, p167). However, during the early Tudor period most ships were built using the more traditional method of lapstrake or clinker building. This is a building technique where sufficient layers of hull planking are overlapped and fastened to each other (Fig 19) by wrought iron nails driven through the overlap, from outboard in, and bent over a rhomboid washer on the inside, called a rove.

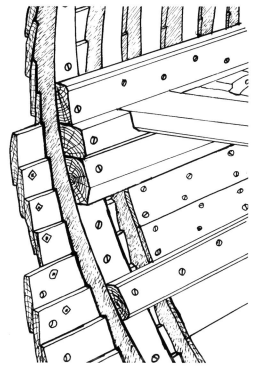

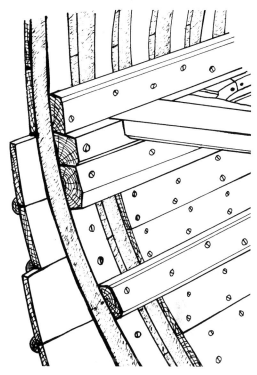

Fig 19 Clinker construction.

Fig 20 Clinker construction of *the Newport ship*.

Fig 21 Carvel construction.

Once successive layers of planking had been built up the framing could be fashioned, placed in the hull and fastened in place. The runs of planks, called strakes, were fastened to the frames by large treenails, often wedged and caulked on the outside. The most extreme example of clinker building is that seen on the river Hamble, and the remains of *Henry Grace à Dieu* (Fig 20), though lighter forms were still being built as seen in the Newport ship (Fig 21). By the end of Henry's VIII reign, clinker-built ships were considered inferior and out of fashion. On 6 August 1545 Suffolk described a number of clinker-built foreign ships brought into Portsmouth as '…both feeble, olde, and out of fashion' (Oppenheim 1896b, p54).

The new fashionable method of shipbuilding was carvel construction. Carvel is where the frames of a ship are first fashioned and fastened in place and the planks then fastened to the frames, but more importantly the planks are laid flush and butted on top of each other (Fig 21). The individual components are fastened together with treenails and large wrought iron nails called spikes, sometimes termed carvel spikes. The planks do not overlap, though might be scarfed to each other end to end. The seams are made watertight by caulking. The caulking consisted of oakum then spun animal hair mixed with tar, and finally in the lower parts of the ship a seam batten. Oakum at this time consisted of old rope or old sailcloth that has been untwisted so it lies in loose strands of flax. A finer form of oakum, called white oakum, was made from loose unprocessed flax. Such white

oakum was placed in the rabbets of the stem and stern posts as well as that of the keel prior to the offering up and fastening of the planks. The tar was a form of processed resin. Henry VII had his two new ships, the *Sovereign* and *Regent*, built in this fashion; there being 'Spykes and Carvell Nayles' made for repairing the *Regent* (Oppenheim 1896a, p228). Interestingly clench nails and roves were used in the repair and construction of their clinker-built ship's boats.

Transom stern

The mounting of guns firing aft in the stern did not require any change in construction, such guns could be fired from the square stern of the summercastle. However, the mounting of large and heavy guns low down in the hull firing out the side of the ship required the width of the ship to be carried to the stern, where it is easiest to terminate in a flattened stern, called a transom stern.

The transom stern (a flat stern), where two curved timbers called fashion pieces projected out of the top of the sternpost, allowed the hull planking to terminate in a strong and deep rabbet. The fashion pieces form the outboard corners of the stern, while the planks of the transom close the stern, running from the fashion piece to the sternpost. The transom planks lie at 45 degrees across the stern and therefore fasten almost at 90 degrees to the edge of the rabbet (Fig 22).

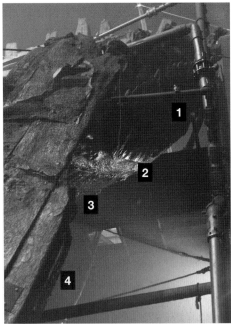

Fig 22 The stern and fashion piece.
1 Transom planking 2 Fashion piece
3 Hull planking 4 Sternpost

Fig 23 Forecastle timbers.

Lidded gunports

No definitive date can be given for the invention of the lidded gunport, and it is unlikely that such a date will ever be found as its appearance was a process of evolution and not invention. Ships were known to have had ports cut into them from the late 15th century onwards. Such ports were found in the stern of large ships and generally considered loading ports which would be closed when the vessel was at sea. By the beginning of the 16th century gunports formed part of the latest naval technology. Tradition states that it was a French shipwright named Descharges who first cut gunports low down in the hull of a ship and fixed lids to them sometime around 1505.

It is known that the French ship *La Cordelère,* c1490s, mounted 16 large guns on its lower deck. To be effective the guns must have been fired through ports, the position of which would require them to have been lidded. King James IV of Scotland was known to be an avid supporter of heavy ordnance and its use on board ships. His enthusiasm culminated in the building of the *Great Michael*, a ship mounting large guns and built by a French shipwright 'Jack Tarrett'. Lord Darcy informed Henry that James spent much of his time on board his ships, numbering 16 to 20 (Oppenheim 1896b, p47). James used his shipborne ordnance to reduce the island fortress of CairnnaBurgh on the Scottish Western Islands, possibly the first such strategic use of shipborne firepower (Guilmartin 2002, p96). That such a nation as Scotland might appear to lead England in the use of such

naval ordnance need not appear surprising, as Scotland and France had a close political relationship known as the 'Auld Alliance'. The *Great Michael* was eventually sold to France while the *La Cordelière* was destroyed by fire during the Battle of Brest in 1512. This was a battle in which the *Mary Rose* and its crew took part and witnessed the burning of the *Regent* and *La Cordelière,* some possibly looking through their own gunports.

The two Great Ships that Henry VIII inherited, the *Regent* and *Sovereign*, while being large and heavily armed with ordnance, did not have lidded gunports. The list of ordnance on board is never mentioned as being on the orlop deck, and there are no mentions of ports or lids or the fittings required for them (Oppenheim, 1896a). In contrast to this, the *Mary Rose* would appear to have had ports cut into her hull when built. In 1511 money was paid '…about the making of pavese and Porte aboard the *Mary Rose…*' Furthermore '…planke of elme for to make the porte in the seide ship…' highlights that they were lidded (McElvogue 2012 and PRO, E 36/12). The context of this statement suggest the ports are built into the ship and form part of the armaments of the ship, and are thus not just ports for ventilation or light. Within a year of this (c1512) a list of things required for making ports for the 'Great Carrack', comprised of ironwork, which included clinker nails and roves used in making the port lids, '…iron and coal to make joints, spikes, clenches for making of the ports…' (Knighton and Loades 2002, p61). It has been suggested that this might refer to the rebuilding of the *Regent* or *Sovereign*; however, both vessels had been rebuilt between 1509 and 1511 and were in active service in 1512 when this document was written. With this evidence it seems reasonable that ports were cut into the main part of the hull and that lids were added to them when the *Mary Rose* was first built and not at a later date, as argued by others (Hildred 2011, p7–8). It is unconceivable that the young Henry would build new ships along old lines when those to the north and south of him were already showing the way.

Building the *Mary Rose*

The first timbers to be fashioned then laid down on the stocks in the building yard, joined and fastened together were the three large baulks of elm that formed the keel of the *Mary Rose*. Once the keel had been made, the floors of the master and quarter frames could be fashioned and placed on the keel, termed 'crossing it'. The floors in-between these could be crossed, their outer shape being checked for fairness with battens. Once the main body of floors had been laid down the keelson was fashioned, having its made-to-measure rebates cut then placed in position and fastened in place with the large wrought iron keel bolts. At the same time the lower part of the stempost with the false stem inside it was fastened in place. The upper parts of the stem could then be raised and fastened in place. The sternpost with the transom was in turn raised and fastened in place, its internal deadwood knee steadying it.

With both stem and stern posts raised the first few planks could be attached, these being the garboard stealers and actual garboards themselves. Each plank was held in place while the large wrought iron carvel spikes were hammered home at either end. After this the holes for the treenails, one per plank per frame, were drilled and the treenails hammered home. In this way the outer hull planking was built up from stem to stern out to the end floors. Once here the next part in the sequence of the framing could be placed in the hull. These would be the bilge futtocks that would carry the shape of the hull from the floors through to the turn of the bilge. Once in place, the lower part of the ceiling planking and the thick stuff could then be made and fastened down. Possibly at this stage the riders were also placed in the ship. The ceiling planking was held in place by treenails that were driven through the hull, one per outer hull plank per frame making at least two treenails per plank per frame. The riders were held in place by large wrought iron bolts. Where the shape of the hull broadens, and space appears between the main series of frames, free floating filler frames were inserted to strengthen the area.

The hull of the *Mary Rose* was built with the next framing sequence being placed after that below where it had been fastened. The timber was used 'as it came', with variations in heights and widths being accepted and dealt with. In this way the hull was built up to the orlop deck. Here, internal deck clamps with shouldering to accept the deck beams define the upper part of the hull. The framing continues with a marked tumblehome above this, but

Fig 25 (left) Looking forwards from Station No 4. Fig 26 (right) A standard and tack holes at the bow.

only to the height of the gunwale. The deck beams below the main or lower orlop sit in a clamp, but they are lighter and does not have any shouldering, being the same as those above the orlop deck. In the waist, the forecastle and the summercastle project forward and aft of the gunwale.

Summercastle

The framing of the summercastle is lighter than that of the main hull. It starts at the orlop deck and extends vertically through the summercastle, upwards from the summer deck, and the middle deck to the poop. The deck below the summer deck is called the 'nether deck', or lower deck, while the forward part of the summer and poop deck is the 'breast' and the aft part the 'stern' (Fig 24). The breast and stern both carried heavy guns by 1545 (BLM/485/1–127).

The planking of the summercastle was made from overlapping clapboard: the boards being cleft from the parent log as opposed to sawn as in weather boards. The upper planks overlap the top edge of the lower plank as in clinker but are fastened directly to the framing behind and not through the land of the adjacent plank. This gives the superstructure a light and watertight construction. Piercing the clapboarding are a number of gunports for swivel guns, c1511. By 1545 many of these had been boarded up and ports cut for large carriage-mounted guns such as culverins. The lower part of the summercastle was reinforced with standards. These were bolted to the frames inboard, clamping and supporting the structure

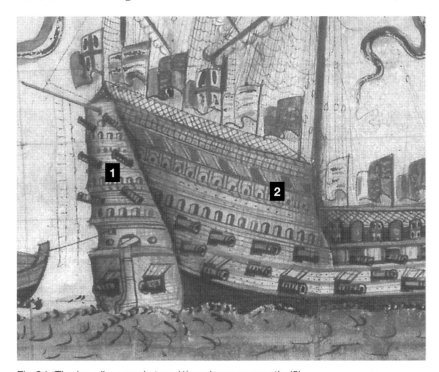

Fig 24 The heavily armed stern (1) and summercastle (2).

between them. The standards also supported the chain wale, which helped spread the shrouds beyond the side of the summercastle and ran from the forward face of the summercastle aft nearly to the stern. A rigging wale ran above the chain wale on the outside of the standards, allowing some of the running and standing rigging to be fastened here.

Forecastle

The forecastle was a deck that projected upwards and forwards over the bows. The area below it was called the nether deck, the aft face of which was defined by a large arch called the cubbridge head. The forecastle of the *Mary Rose* had two full-length covered decks, the forecastle itself and the 'deck above' the forecastle. Above this was another full-length deck only half of which was covered. The upper part was called the 'highest deck'. The forecastle was triangular in shape, the aft face of which above the 'cubbridge head' was called the 'barbican'. The lower two decks of the barbican had gunports for guns firing aft to cover the waist.

The waist

The area between the summercastle and the forecastle was called the 'waist'. Either side of the waist of the *Mary Rose* was lined with pavises. Originally these were the shields of knights and men-at-arms positioned along the sides of the ship, but later became light wooden boards positioned between a parallel pair of horizontal rails. The pavises provided close quarter protection for the troops and gun crews in the waist. They were removable, allowing archers and hand gunners to fire out between them, and to allow boarders to stream across onto an opposing deck. Covering the inboard part of the waist was anti-boarding netting (Fig 27), supported on beams held up along the centreline by 'T'-shaped supports.

Braces and riders

Listed for the *Sovereign* in the inventories of Henry VII are:

'...Tymbre of hym bought in grete occupied and spent under the Ovyloppes and Alawe in the seid Ship for to fortifie and bynde her stronge...' (Oppenheim 1896a, p176).

That is to say: '...large timber bought to be used under and below the orlop deck to help bind and make it strong'. This aptly describes the braces, be they diagonal or vertical, which run from under the orlop and below to the bottom of the ship at the end of the riders. The riders were heavy internal floors fastened over the keelson and ceiling planking under each deck beam.

Decks

The decks are defined by large oak beams (12 in all) from stem to stern. The beams are let into shouldered rebates along the deck clamps, a heavy stringer running fore and aft. At main deck and orlop deck height the beams

Fig 27 Netting being made.

are supported by standing knees, only the main deck is supported by lodging knees and a deck clamp that has shouldering around the rebates. Running fore and aft either side of the masts and rebated into the deck beams are two lines of carlings. Ledges extend from the sides of the ship to the carlings, and from each row of carlings to the other. The central ledges of the orlop deck and lower orlop, are not fastened to the carlings only to the short planks above them, which allow them to be removed thus acting as hatches. Just as the framing of the summercastle and forecastle is lighter than the hull framing, so are the decks. The orlop deck was made of 2in elm board while the lower orlop was 1½in, the waist and nether decks 1in and the forecastle and summercastle and above of 1in. All the decks from the orlop and above are caulked. At the aft end of the waist was the dale, aft of which the nether deck steps down.

Pumps, dailes, gutters and scuppers

The *Mary Rose* was originally fitted with two pumps, one beside the mainmast and the other aft beside the mizzen. Both pump tubes were made from boring out an elm trunk, fitting a leather one-way valve to the bottom and another at the end of a long spear. The spear is forced up and down by the use of a brake attached to a crook at the top of the tube. The pump of the *Sovereign* was used in the dock at Portsmouth and is described as having 'Minches with a swivell a bolte and Ryng...' (Oppenheim 1896a, p157). The top of the tube is left open for the water to flow out. A manger gathered the

Fig 28 The last two gunports on the main orlop deck.

little in the preceding years apart from more detail being added. A building specification for the *Mary Rose*, as seen on page 22, could therefore be expected to follow the same format.

References

British Library (BL) M/485/1–127

Friel, I, *The Good Ship: Ships, Shipbuilding and Technology in England, 1200–1520,* British Museum Press, 1995

Guilmartin, JF in Gardiner, R (Ed), *Cogs, Caravels and Galleons: the sailing ship 1000–1650,* Conway's History of the Ship, 1994

Guilmartin, JF, *Galleons and Galleys,* Cassell & Co., 2002

Hildred, A (Ed), *Weapons of Warre: The armament of the Mary Rose,* Archaeology of the Mary Rose, Vol 3, 7–8, Mary Rose Trust, 2011

M^{C}Elvogue, DM, *101 questions about the Mary Rose,* PRO E 36/12, 2012

Oppenheim, M, *A History of the Administration of the Royal Navy 1509–1660,* 1896b

water as it flowed out of the top and guided it to the daile. The dailes, one for each pump, were oak U-shaped channels that allowed the water to flow out either side of the ship. On the breast of the summercastle and barbican there were also gutters. The scuppers, three per side along the orlop deck, were pre-drilled square tubes let into the side of the ship between the frames and were caulked on the outside. Around the outer scupper hole was nailed a leather sleeve, which acted as a one-way valve, closing off the scuppers when they were immersed when the ship heeled. To allow the water to run to the scuppers, on the orlop deck, the standing knees had waterways cut into them. The nether, summer and poop decks all have waterways along the side of the hull but no scupper holes. Instead the water ran down the decks to the gutters where it was then let out of the ship.

Fastenings

All the elements of the ship (apart from a few notable exceptions) are held together by large treenails. Where extra strength was deemed necessary, such as the keel and stem/stern post fastenings, wrought iron bolts were used. Nails and spikes of varying sizes were also used throughout the ship. The size and shape of the fastening is often dependent on the nature of its use. Spikes were generally used on the ship's hull while nails were used on ancillary parts such as decking, tingles and partitioning.

The building specification

The earliest building specification (16 May/ 3 June 1589) discovered to date is that for the *Merahonora* built by Mathew Baker. The specification changes

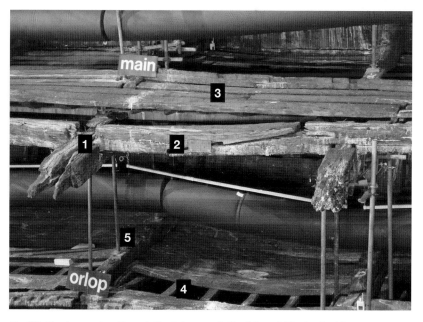

Fig 29 Deck construction. 1 Deck beam 2 Caulking 3 Deck planking
4 Ledges 5 Standards

Building specifications for *Mary Rose*

A note of the manner how the new Great Ship to be called the *Mary Rose* determined to be made by the King, to be in the order of 500 tons shall be ordered and thoroughly performed and finished.

1 The ship shall be 100ft long on the touch of the keel, 38ft broad between beam ends and 13ft deep under the beam of the main orlop to the top of the keel.

2 From the keel at 8ft height to have 12 beams well bound to lay a false orlop of 1in elm board so far as need shall require, under which 12 beams must be 12 riders well bolted, and where the riders besides the footwales must have sufficient sleepers on every side fore and aft, and the pillars to be bolted sufficiently, the ground timbers and futtocks to be 14in deep and the 'posse' answerable in bigness of white sound and perfect oak.

3 The main orlop to have 12 beams well bound with side knees and standards, every knee having at least two bolts, and this orlop to be laid with 3in planks of sound and seasoned oak and caulked.

4 The second overlop to be well bound and laid with sound and seasoned 2in oak plank, and to be well bound with side knees and standards, every knee having at least two bolts.

5 The half-deck to the mast to be well bound and laid with 2in oak plank, to be well bound with side knees and hanging and every knee to have at least two bolts.

6 To have a forecastle and a barbican to the mast and other buildings above to fit the ship with comeliness.

7 The main capstan to go allow the cat to be fair upon that orlop forward with a pair of carrack bitts.

8 The jeer capstan to be made aloft in the waist, and the cubbridge heads to be made musket free with elm board,

9 The outside of the ship from the keel to the second wale to be wrought with 4in plank, and so much thereof as shall be above water to be dry stuff and seasoned from the upper wale to the quick side or waist to be dry 3in plank.

10 Above the waist to be 1¼in plank, cleft and fastened direct to the frames, and the rails to be inboard to go to the ship's side; the ship to be painted from 2ft above the chainwales, upward with colours in oil; to be carved likewise and garnished with gold, with galleries about the stern and casement as is fit for such a ship.

11 The making of two ovens and paving the kitchen likewise to be set up and the cook room to be done effectually below the false overloppe in the hold of the said ship. The steward rooms, rope room and powder room to be fully furnished with such cabins before every of them as hath been usual, and the bread room to be sealed on the false overloppe of the said ship.

12 Cabins to be made upon the lower orlop for the boatswain, the purser, the surgeon and the carpenter, and the quartermaster's cabin where it may be best placed by the bitts; the gunner's room likewise, and cabins therein where places may be had, and elsewhere upon that orlop where it may be thought convenient.

13 Cabins likewise to be made upon the second orlop for the company as place will

suffer, and as shall be thought convenient by the lord admiral or the officers of the navy, together with a cabin abaft by the mizzen for the boatswain's mates.

14 The captain's cabin and the master's to be so wrought as they may be sealed to the plank with spruce deals or wainscot for avoiding of mice and rats, and that such windows be therein made as shall be thought fit by the lord admiral or the officers. The steerage likewise to be wrought and sealed with spruce deals, and a dining room for the captain, garnished and to be furnished with locks, bolts, hinges etc, and such cabins to be made before the steerage and the master's cabin as shall be thought fit by the lord admiral or the officers.

15 The ship to be sufficiently bound with knees, both standards and side knees, where it shall be thought meet, and that the beams be of a sufficient scantling, and the clamps to be 8in thick, the chainwales, wales and rails to be of a sufficient scantling, and with an edge above the flat for the better caulking. The hull is to fortified and bound under the orloppes and below, with timber to brace it and make it strong.

16 All the bolts and spikes, rudder irons and hinges for ports to be of Spanish iron, and the bolts under the chainwale to be of 1¼in through, and above that 1¼in through, and more or less, as shall be thought meet by the lord admiral or officers of the navy.

17 The ship to be caulked with a thread of oakum and a thread of hair thorough out and perfect 'puppett' oakum of hemp under the wales, in the rabbet of the stems, sternpost, keel and transoms, as shall be thought meet by the lord admiral or the officers, and about the wales sufficiently as the place shall require.

18 A new boat and a cock boat to be made sufficient and answerable in service for such a ship.

19 That all the masts and yards be made, fitted, set and closed up; and if there be not masts great enough, then to have the spills at her majesty's charge, and to make them up with oak.

20 All the ports to be furnished with ring bolts, and all such as be upon the lower orlop or elsewhere that hath a demi-culverin, port piece, cannon or above to have four ring bolts to a port, the rest two ring bolts to a port, with shackles and rings accordingly.

21 One main pump besides the mainmast step in the belly of the ship and another ordinary pump in the buttocks of the ship, beside the mizzen mast.

All shall be wrought with good effect for the purpose of the King.
Written at Portsmouth, the 16th day of the month of May in the second year of our lord's reign.

By your own Robert Brigandine, Clerk of the Ships.

The building contract for the Mary Rose *is based on one by the famous Elizabethan shipwright Mathew Baker, dated 16 May 1589. The ship is not dissimilar in size to the* Mary Rose. *The original layout and terms of the specification are used, but with the dimensions and features of the ship of 1589 replaced by those of the* Mary Rose *and signed Robert Brigandine as opposed to Mathew Baker.*

Original design concept

A1   Rising lines

A2   Narrowing lines

A3   Keel line

A4   Position for the master mould

A5   Master and quarter moulds, stempost and transom

1   Transom
2   Quarter mould
3   Master mould
4   Keel
5   Quarter mould
6   Stem

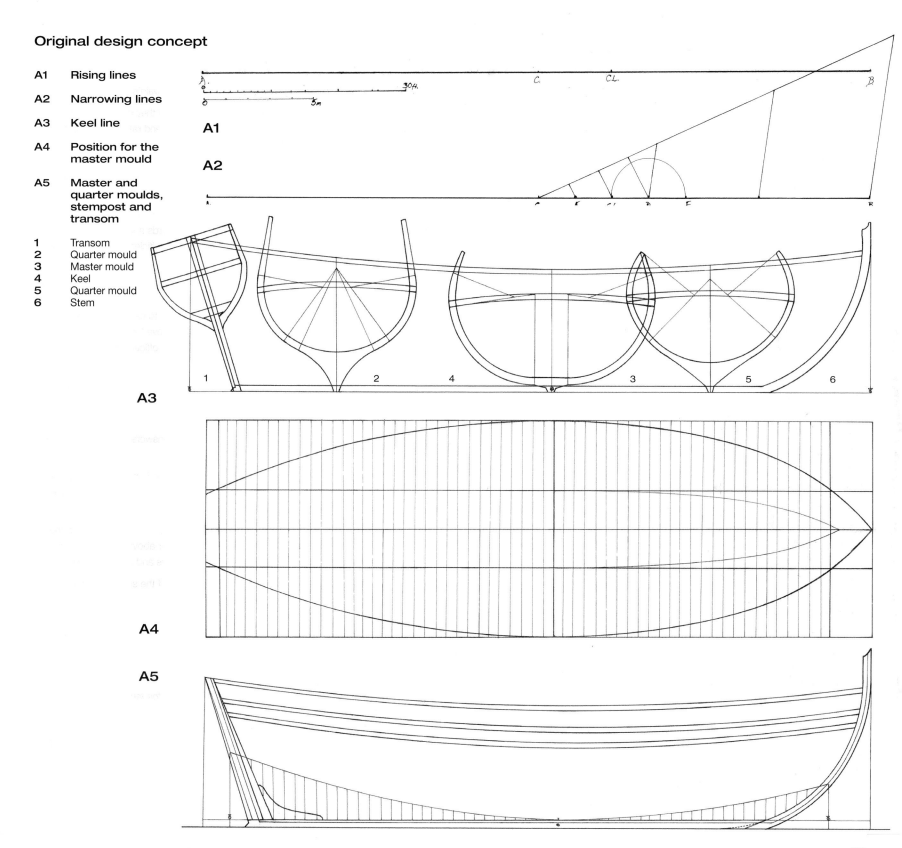

A1

A2

A3

A4

A5

3 FITTING OUT THE MARY ROSE

'…all manner of implements necessaries to the same two ships…'(Knighton and Loades 2002, p7).

Fitting out a ship usually means making and fitting into the hull all the parts that are required to allow it to sail and work, such as the masts and rigging. For a man-o-war it also meant all the paraphernalia with which to fight; including the breeching rings, breeching ropes and the ordnance itself stocked and or lashed onto their gun carriage. The *Mary Rose* was built at Portsmouth and hallowed in 1511 before having her masts raised and being fitted out,

'…for all manner of implements necessaries to the same two ships belonging as particularly ensueth, first for sails, twine, marline, ropes, cables, cablets, shrouds, hawsers, buoy ropes, stays, sheets, buoy lines, tacks, lifts, top armours, streamers, standards, compasses, running glasses, tankards, bowls, dishes, lanterns, shivers of brass and pulleys for the said two new ships, victuals and wages of men for setting up of their masts, shrouds and all other tacklings for the said two new ships…' (Knighton and Loades 2002, p7).

Fig 32 A pot for boiling pitch.

Ship's equipment

The *Mary Rose* was equipped not only with her arms and armaments, sails, masts and rigging but also the equipment needed to navigate her and to feed her crew. In the lists are all manner of equipment considered necessary for the ship when fitted out, including compasses and running glasses, both of which were needed for navigating the ship, even if only for piloting it along the coast. To sound the watches and call the men to station, the ship was also issued with a bell (Fig 30). To feed the crew the King provided his ships with tankards, bowls and dishes, while he also issued the ship with lanterns so that the crew could see in the dark parts of the ship (like the hold) and at night (Fig 31).

Masts and yards

The *Mary Rose* had four masts mentioned in the inventories: the main, fore, mizzen and bonaventure mizzen. The first two provide the main propulsion and the latter two help to balance the ship and steer her. The bowsprit is included in inventories. The mainmast was stepped on the keelson, the foremast on the orlop deck, the mizzen on the forecastle deck and the bonaventure on the upper deck.

Mainmast

In 1514 the mainmast of the *Mary Rose* consisted of the main, top and top gallant masts and was rigged with main, main top and top gallant yards. The mainmast was composite, the foot of which sat in a rebate in the keelson called the mast step. At deck level the mast was supported by a pair

Fig 30 The ship's bell.

Fig 31 A lantern.

of partners, two beams lying athwartship and bolted to the carlings either side of the mast with wrought iron bolts. They were rebated to accept the mast. The mast was at least 2ft 6in if not 3ft 2in in diameter at its step and tapered upwards towards the orlop deck. Its core was of oak, 2ft 3in by 2ft 3in with at least eight further oak timbers bound to it. It would appear from a document of c1538 that the mast was at least 150ft long. On 21 March 1538 Lovedaye wrote to Wriothesley saying that 'There is making for the Admiral a ship of the fashion as the *Peterpomegarnet*, but greater. Her mast is 150ft long' (Marsden 2003, p7). There were only two ships contemporary with this document that were of the same fashion as but greater in size than the *Peter Pomegranate*, the *Mary Rose* and *Henry Grace à Dieu*. The old practice or ratio for the diameter of the one-masted ship was 1in in diameter for the mast for every foot of beam, which would make it 3ft 2in in diameter (Laughton 1932, p93).

Foremast

The foremast is smaller than the main and was the second mast listed, and offered further motive power. In this period it was stepped well forward at orlop deck level above the keel to stem scarf or on the stem. In 1514 the foremast had a main and topmast crossed with main and top yards.

Main mizzen

The main mizzen consisted of a mainmast and a topmast both crossed with main and top yards.

Bonaventure mizzen

The bonaventure mizzen appears in the latter part of the15th century. It is used to help balance the effects of the superstructure most notably the highly charged forecastles of the Great Ships. This is succinctly put by the unknown author of a treatise on rigging c1625 formerly at Petworth House:

'Somme ships have two missons ether regard of ther length of qualeties…' and continues:
'In regard of ther qualety is when a ship will not keepe the winde and that her head falles of, which is incident to all ships hie built…' (Salisbury and Anderson 1958).

Thus the bonaventure allowed the highly charged ships to sail to windward more effectively. An 'outligger' extended aft beyond the stern to allow the clew of the sail to be fully sheeted. In 1514 the *Mary Rose* had a bonaventure mast fitted with a yard.

Bowsprit

The bowsprit was a mast or long spar that projected forwards and upwards at an angle of about 40 degrees over the stem. In 1514 it consisted of the bowsprit itself crossed with a yard.

Standing rigging

Each mast has its own standing rigging. The mainmast and foremast are nearly identical while the main and bonaventure mizzens are rigged in a similar but less numerous fashion. The bowsprit standing rigging is more peculiar, having no shrouds but instead relied on the strength of the bowsprit and a number of stays running aft to the foremast. The main and mizzen masts' standing rigging is spread by a timber shelf called a 'channel' running along the side of the summercastle. Below this is the chain wale, into which the bolts at the lower end of the chains are fastened, and above which was a rigging rail to which the rigging could be lashed or tied. A similar channel also ran aft from the forecastle along the side of the ship allowing the crew to serve the main tack, sheets and possibly even the bowlines. The bonaventure mizzen and foremast standing rigging was fastened higher up on the superstructure. The general arrangement of the mainmast standing rigging is described as: '…a stay, a schyrwyn, 26 shrouds, 26 iron chains with bolts pertaining to them, eight swifting tackles, eight polancres, three garlands.'

Fig 33 The shrouds.

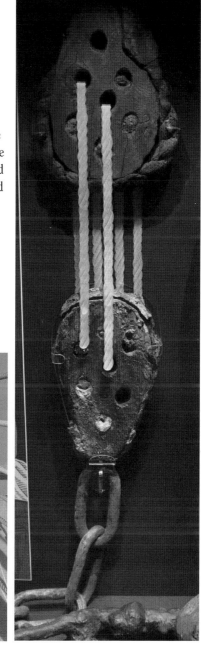

Fig 34 A chainplate and blocks.

Mainstay and schyrwyn

The mainstay ran forward from the top of the mainmast down into the forecastle and to the stem where it was fastened. There was no backstay. The schyrwyn remains a mystery but might be some form of swifting tackle to accompany the forestay.

Fig 36 Mast parrell.

Fig 37 Clew garnets.

Fig 35 Various blocks and sheaves.

Fig 38 Pendant blocks.

Shrouds

Shrouds, also called head ropes, run from the top of the mainmast to the sides of the ship. In 1514 there appear to be 13 a side while in 1545 there were 10 (Fig 33). Each shroud, a rope 2in in diameter, was attached to the top of the mainmast and its lower end fastened around a deadeye. The deadeye along with its partner below had seven holes through which a ¾in diameter lanyard was laced and tightened. The lower deadeye, around which was an iron strap, was in turn fastened to the upper wale by a chain and bolt.

Swifting tackles and polancres

The shrouds were supported by swifters and polancres. The swifters consisted of a series of blocks and tackles attached to a pendant fastened around the top of the masthead below the shrouds. They extended down to the rigging rail where a lower pendant fastened the lower tackles to the

rigging rail. The lanyard, which when hauled in tightened the swifters, was also fastened to the rigging rail. The swifter appears to have been fastened before the shrouds where they could be slacked when the yards were braced round when sailing to windward. Just as we do not know what schyrwyn are, we do not know what polancres are (Howard, p30); though they appear to go out of use (in the records at least) during the first part of the 16th century.

Garlands

Mentioned for the mainmast are a set of garlands. Mainwaring, writing in 1644, describes these as '…a rope about the mainmast-head which is called a collar or a garland, and is there placed to save the shrouds from galling' (Mainwaring, p129), others consider them to be iron bands that helped to hold the topmast to the mainmast (Howard, p30). In later periods they are replaced by caps and tressletrees.

Fig 39 A fighting top.

Sails

The *Mary Rose* had a full set of sails. On the mainmast there was a main course and two bonnets, a topsail and a top gallant. This was mirrored on the foremast with a fore course with two bonnets and a fore topsail, but no fore top gallant. The main mizzen had a mizzen sail and topsail, while the bonaventure had a mainsail only. The bowsprit had a single spritsail. Spare sails and bonnets were carried in the store in the forward part of the lower orlop deck.

The sails were made from lengths of cloth stitched together lengthwise. The cloth was made from hemp (Fig 40), possibly including nettle fibre and was

Fig 40 Tudor sailcloth.

Rigging indenture 9 August 1514

...parcels of stuff ensuing out of the Mary Rose.

That is to say, first a mainmast, a main yard, 2 courses to the mainsail, 2 bonnets to the same, 2 tacks, 2 sheets, 2 bowlines, a parrell, 2 trusses, 2 thrings, 2 brasses (braces) and a pair of ties, a winding halyard, 2 lifts, a gear, a stay, a schyrwyn, 26 shrouds, 26 iron chains with bolts pertaining to them, 8 swifting tackles, 8 polancres and 3 garlands.

Item the main top, a topmast and a maintop yard, the parrell, a main topsail, 2 bowlines, 2 sheets, 2 lifts, 2 brasses, a tie, a halyard, and a stay, with 10 shrouds and a truss.

Item the topgallant, a mast, a sail, a yard with the parrell, 2 bowlines, 2 sheets, 2 brasses, 2 lifts and a stay with 6 shrouds.

Item the foremast, a yard, the parrell, a course, with 3 bonnets, 2 tacks, 2 sheets, 2 bowlines, 2 lifts, 2 brasses, 2 trusses, 16 shrouds, 16 iron chains with their bolts, 4 pulleys, a stay, 2 ties, a halyard.

Item foretop, the topmast, a yard, a sail, 2 bowlines, 2 sheets, 2 lifts, 2 brasses, a tie, a halyard, a stay and a parrell.

Item the bowsprit, a yard, a spritsail and a bonnet, a truss and a pair of lifts.

The main mizzen mast and his yard, a parrell, the sail, a tie and a halyard, a truss, a sheet, 2 brasses, a lift, a stay, 12 shrouds and 12 iron chains with their bolts.

Item the main mizzen topmast, a yard and parrell, the sail and truss, a lift and 8 shrouds.

Item a bonaventure mast with the yard, the parrelll, 2 sails, a tie, a halyard, a truss, a sheet, a stay and 8 shrouds.

a coarse weave. Along the upper and lower edge a bolt rope was attached while the edges of the sail had a leech rope. Along the lower edge a number of cringles were sewn so that the bonnets could be laced to the sail.

Running rigging

To handle and control the sails and yards the *Mary Rose* had a series of ropes, pulleys and blocks. There were two main forms of running rigging, one which controlled the yards and the other the sails.

The fore and aft position of the yards was controlled by braces, which ran through a block attached to the end of the yard by a pennant and ran aft.

The yards were held to the masts by a parrell (Fig 36), two trusses and thrings. They were raised up the mast by the ties, halyards and jeers. The ties went from the yard to the top of the mast, over a pulley and down to a block behind the mast. Threaded through this block and its pair was a halyard that was wound in around a windlass, otherwise known as 'a gear'. A set of jeers were also fitted. These consisted of a block on the yard with another at the front of the masthead with the halyard leading down the front of the mast. Two lifts were attached, one at each end of the yard helping to haul the yards up and control the angle that the yard lay. A truss was used to help haul the yards down.

The bottoms of the sails were controlled by a sheet, which ran aft and a tack that ran forwards. They ran through blocks attached to the corner of the sails by a pendant. Further up each side of the sail was attached a bowline (Fig 38). This helped to pull the forward edge of the sail into the wind, refilling the sail when tacking and holding it in position when sailing close into the wind, called by contemporaries 'hard on a bowline'. To depower the sail, a number of ropes attached to the centre of the sail led around the mast and back to the sail then down to the deck. They helped spill the wind out of the centre of the sail.

To help furl the sail, bunt lines were attached down the centre of the sail, with brailing ropes at either side of these. These were attached to the lower edge, then went up over the yard and back down the sail to the deck. Hauling on them thus drew the sail up. Martinets, otherwise known as leech line bridles, helped to gather in the side of the sail while clew lines, which were fitted to the bottom corner of the sail, gathered it up from there. Though not suggested in the official Mary Rose Trust Archaeological volume (Marsden 2009), evidence for clew lines comes from the clew garnets (clew blocks on pennets) listed in the inventories (Oppenheim 1896a), and the blocks recovered from the excavation (Fig 37).

Decking out
The last part of fitting out the ship was to decorate and arm it. This was not done in Portsmouth but on the River Thames, London. At least 24 soldiers dressed in green and white coats accompanied the *Mary Rose* on its journey to the Thames (Knighton and Loades 2002, p8). Once in the Thames, apart from stocking and fitting the ordnance on board (see arming and fighting on page 31), the *Mary Rose* was decked out with streamers, banners, top armours and standards:

'…indenture for all manner of stuff needful to be had for the decking … of the same ship' (Knighton and Loades 2002, p9).

In this context 'decking' does not mean the boards for the ships decks but instead decked as in decoration.

Both the master (Thomas Sperte) and the purser (David Boner) were paid for rigging and decking the ship. This probably means the purser bought and paid for the material and possibly oversaw the making of the individual banners, streamers and standards, while the master oversaw the rigging required to hang the streamers and banners. Before any of the streamers or banners could be hung they had to be painted and stained. This was done by the painter John Browne of London, who was paid £142 4s, 6d for:

'…painting and staining certain banners and streamers for use of our ships called the *Mary Rose* and *Peter Pomegranate*…' (Knighton and Loades, p9).

The streamers and banners were made from:

'…tukes, buckrams, Brussels cloths and camlets…' (Knighton and Loades, p9),

such material being bought from the London 'mercer' William Botry. Tukes were a certain type of canvas made from hemp or flax, while buckram was a stiff course linen cloth in general use at the time. Brussels cloth is a twill or corded fabric made from wool or cotton and wool. Camlets was now considered an inferior cloth. During Tudor times it was a fine oriental woven material made from camel hair.

Tudor flags and ensigns
The *Mary Rose* was fitted out with a full set of flags, banners, streamers and guidons. It was during Tudor times that the St George's flag became the recognised distinguishing flag of both English warships and merchantmen. Apart from the St George's Cross the predominant emblems were mainly religious or heraldic, which were repeated in different forms. The heraldic forms were based on the ship owner's, captain's or monarch's heraldic crests

Flags, streamers, banners, guidons and pennants 9 August 1514

Mary Rose carried the following flags: '…a banner of St Katherine in metall: 5 banners of the arms of Boulonge in metall; 4 banners of the Rose and Pomegranite in metall; one of St Peter in metall; 2 of the Castell in metall; 1 streamer of St George in colour; 1 streamer of the red lyon in colour; 1 streamer of the Castell in colour.' The *Mary Rose* carried 18 banner staves (PM vol 1 p170)

Anthony Roll 1546

Bonaventure

Masthead	Flag – St George's Cross and green
Fighting top	Streamer – St George's Cross and green and white fly

Flags, streamers, banners, guidons and pennants

(No scale)

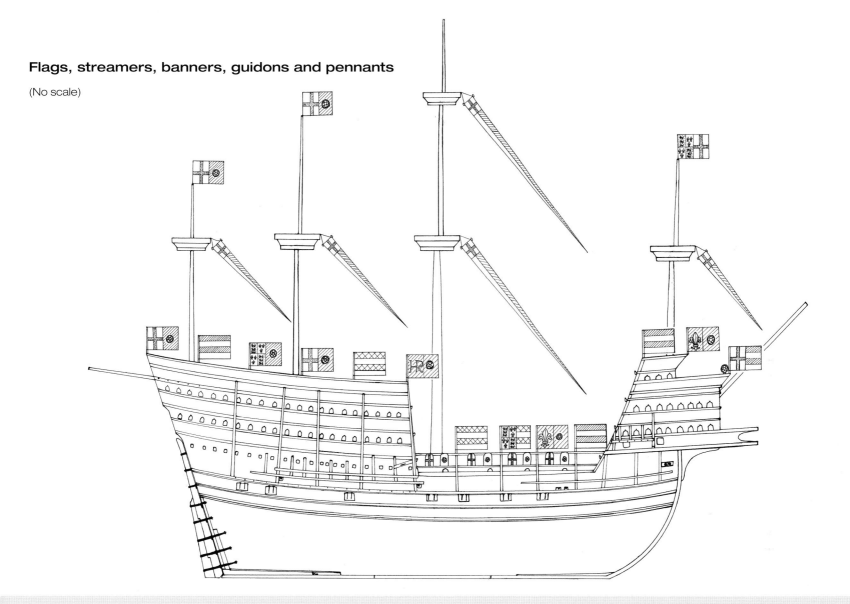

Mizzen		Aft castle	St George's Cross and Tudor Rose on green, green and silver horizontal stripes, Royal Standard and green, St George's Cross and green, white and yellow horizontal stripes, HR halved with Tudor Rose on green
Masthead	Flag – St George's Cross and green		
Fighting top	Streamer – St George's Cross and green and white fly		
Main			
Masthead	Flag – St George's Cross and green	Waist	Green and white horizontal stripes, single Fleur De Lys on green, yellow and white horizontal stripes, white and yellow halved with Royal Banner
Fighting top	Streamer – St George's Cross and green and white fly		
Fore			
Masthead	Flag – Council banner, Royal Standard halved with St George's Cross	Pavise	St George's Cross between Tudor Rose on green
Fighting top	Streamer – St George's Cross and green and white fly	Forecastle	Yellow and silver horizontal stripes, green and silver horizontal stripes, single Fleur de Lys on green/blue, St George's Cross halved with silver and green horizontal stripes
Bowsprit	Nothing		

Fig 41 Waist deck flags from the Anthony Roll image.

Painting

The *Mary Rose* was painted some time before the spring of 1512. On 5 April, John Browne, the London painter, was paid for delivering '*stuff*' to the ship and for painting the *Mary Rose,* as well as others ships (Marsden 2003, p151). After being decked out and painted and apart from some minor things, costing but 29 shillings and 1½ pence (Knighton and Loades 2002, p9), the *Mary Rose* was ready for her guns.

References

Howard, F, *Sailing Ships of War 1400–1860*, Conway Maritime Press, 1979

Laughton, LG Carr, *Early Masts*, The Mariner's Mirror, Vol 18 1 p93, 1993

Mainwaring, GE (Ed), *The Life and Works of Sir Henry Mainwaring*, The Council of the Navy Records Society, 1920

Purves, AA, *Flags for Ship Modellers and Marine Artists*, Conway Maritime Press, 1983

Salisbury, W and Anderson, RC, *A treatise on shipbuilding: And a treatise on rigging, written about 1620–1625*, Society for Nautical Research, 1958

and badges, while the religious emblems were often that of the patron saint of home ports, the named saint of the ship, while the streamers and standards were decorative and/or emblematic (Purves, p12).

During this period the question of appointment was more important than that of rank. Thus the second and third in command of any fleet were the Vice-Admiral and Rear-Admiral respectively and flew their flags accordingly (Purves, p40). The Lord Admiral flew the Royal Standard at the main and St George's Cross at the fore. The Admiral of the Van was to fly two St George's Flags, one at the main and one at the fore while the Admiral of the Wing St George's Flags at the main mizzen and bonaventure mizzen.

Flags

In 1514 the *Mary Rose* was decked out with 13 banners and three streamers, many of which represented the heraldry of Catherine, Henry's new wife. These included banners of St Katherine, the Rose and Pomegranate of Castell. By the end of his reign, the *Mary Rose* was only decked out in the King's heraldry as is listed on the previous page. The flags consisted of banners and streamers, long flags set at the mastheads, and the 'guidons' or 'gittons' which were deck banners. There was also a pennon that was to be positioned above the forecastle on a staff inclining forwards. It was emblazoned with the devices and colours of the king, or in the case of the *Mary Rose* a red rose as seen in the Anthony Roll.

4 ARMING AND FIGHTING THE MARY ROSE

'…as also the ordenaunce, artillery, munitions and habillimentes for the warre for the armyng of evry of them and for theyr deffence agaynst theyr ennymys apon the see…' (Knighton and Loades 2000, p41).

Fig 42 An orlop deck gun port.

The *Mary Rose* was designed from concept as a ship to be armed with large heavy guns on the main deck, known as the orlop or lower orlop, firing through ports that were lidded (Fig 42) to stop them shipping seas when the guns were not in use. As such she brought in a new era of naval warfare for the English Royal Navy. Paramount to the success of this new fighting system was the ordnance itself, its associated munitions and fittings as well as tools and spares termed 'habiliments of war'.

The guns are the primary part of the system. The *Mary Rose* was not fitted with her armament until she was conveyed to the Thames, in the summer of 1511. By 1 October the gunmaker Cornelius Johnson had been paid for:

'…the new stocking and repairing of divers pieces of [our *inserted*] ordnance of [the King's *deleted*] four of our ships now being in Thames, the one called the *Mary and John*, the other the *Anne* of London, the other the *Mary Rose* and another the *Peter Pomegranate* – £20' (Knighton and Loades 2002, p9).

We are also told that Cornelius is paid:
'…for 8 loads of elm for stocking of the said ordnance, at 4s the load – 32s'.

Only the large guns would need to be stocked as the smaller guns were held in wrought iron minches. There is no reference to cutting portholes or fitting port lids at this stage, therefore we can conclude they were cut at Portsmouth during the making of the ship and prior to her being transported around to the Thames.

The ordnance and artillery

The *Mary Rose*, like all warships, went through a continued series of refits to keep her up to date with the latest technology in armaments, in this respect her ordnance (Fig 43). We do not have the original specifications for fitting out the ship nor a complete inventory of her armaments when she was launched. From 1514, just three years after her launching, an inventory of guns left on board and in the charge and custody of John Browne the master and John Bryarley the purser. This inventory shows a ship armed with a significant level of heavy guns (Great Curtows and Great Murders) that must have been positioned on the lower orlop, or main deck. A 'Grete Curtowes' (curtal) was a large gun considered to be short in relation to its bore, and firing a shot of up to 40lbs.

Fig 43 A replica port piece at Fort Nelson Royal Armoury.

Wrought iron

Iron guns came in both cast and wrought form, with the latter being the most numerous in this period. Wrought iron guns were on the whole breech loading guns, supplied with at least three breech chambers per gun. They came in a range of different sizes from the large stone firing guns and serpentines mounted on wheeled sledges made of elm; to the smaller murders mounted on Y-shaped iron crocks/yokes called 'minches'. Most fired stone shot, though all could fire cast iron round shot and the smaller guns lead shot or pellets.

The Anthony Roll Inventory – 1546
The *Mary Rose*

Tunage – *vijc*

Men [souldiours – clxxxv; marrynars – cc; gonnars – xxxti]: *iiijcxv*

For the Mary Rose. Ordenaunce, artillary, munitions, habillimentes for the warre, for the armyng and in the deffence of the sayd shyppe to the see

Gonnes of brasse
Cannons – *ij*
Demy cannons – *ij*
Culveryns – *ij*
Demy culveryns – *vj*
Sakers – *ij*
Fawcons – *j*
Somma – *xv*

Gonnes of yron
Porte pecys – *xij*
Slynges – *ij*
Dewy slynges – *iiij*
Quarter slyng – *j*
Fowlers – *vj*
Baessys – *xxx*
Toppe pecys – *ij*
Hayle shotte pecys – *xxti*
Handgonnes complete – *l*

Gonnepowder
Serpentyn powder in barrelles – *ij last*
Corne powder in barrelles – *iij*

Shotte of yron
For cannon – *l*
For demy cannon – *lx*
For culveryn – *lx*
For demy culveryn – *cxl*
For sakers – *lxxx*
For fawcon – *lx*
For slyng – *xl*
For demy slyng – *xl*

For qwarter slyng – *l*
Dyce of yron for hayle shotte – *[blank]*

Shotte of stoen and leade
For porte pecys – *cc*
For fowlers – *clxx*
For toppe pecys – *xx*
For baessys, shotte of leade – *iiijc*
For handgonnes, shotte of leade – *jm*

Bowes, bowestrynges, arrowes, morrys pyckes, byllys, daertes for toppis
Bowes of yough – *ccl*
Bowestrynges – *vj groce*
Livere arrowes in shevis – *cccc*
Morrys pykes – *cl*
Byllys – *cl*
Daertes for toppys in doussens – *xl*

Munitions
Pyckehamers – *xij*
Sledgys of yron – *viij*
Crowes of yron – *xij*
Comaunders – *xij*
Tampions – *iiijml*
Canvas for cartowches – *xxti ellys*
Paper ryall for cartowches – *j qwayer*
Fourmes for cartowches – *vj*

Habillimentes for warre
Ropis of hempe for woling and brechyng – *x coylles*
Naylis of sundere sortes – *jml*
Bagges of ledder *viij*
Fyrkyns with pursys *vj*
Lyme pottes – *x doussen*
Spaer whelys – *iiij payer*
Spaer truckelles – *iiij payer*
Spaer extrys – *vj*
Shepe skynnys for spongys – *xij*
Tymber for forlockes and koynnys – *c foete*

Wrought iron guns were made by forming a barrel made from wrought iron bars or a rolled iron sheet held together by wrought iron rings shrunk around it. A second layer of rings was sometimes added to this. The larger gun barrels were mounted on an elm bed hollowed out and fitted with a pair of wheels allowing it to be run out for firing. At the breech end the bed was hollowed to allow for the breech chamber, primed with gunpowder and held in place with a timber breech wedge. The smaller guns were fitted with trunions and a wrought iron breech chamber, which held the breech block and tapered backwards into a tiller. A minch was fastened around the trunions allowing the gun to be mounted on the gun rails in the castles. The guns were fired via a touch hole in the breech chamber, which once fired could quickly be exchanged for another loaded chamber. Consequently each gun was fitted with more than one breech chamber.

Port pieces

Of particular interest are the port pieces. These are large wrought iron breech loading guns that only appear in the inventories from 1535 onwards, weigh about 1,200lb and have a bore between 6 and 10in in diameter and weight of shot between 9 and 10lb. There are none in the 1514 inventory while by 1545 there are 12 listed in the Anthony Roll. In the early part of the 15th century the type of gun used on board ships was not uniform and did not conform to any rating system, being the weapons from the king's personal armoury. Further to this, the names of guns varied throughout this period. Murders are generally thought to be small swivel guns, but their

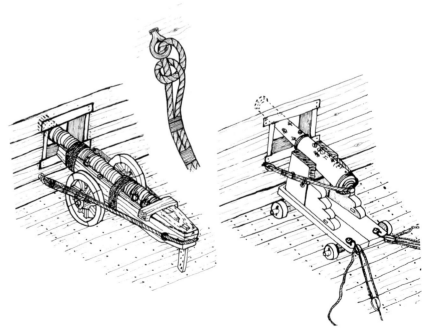

Fig 44 Breeching the heavy ordnance.

description in 1514 classes them as 'grett peces' (great pieces), implying they were large. Therefore it can plausibly be surmised that the introduction of the term 'port piece' along with 'cannon' in the 1540s and the demise of 'curtow' and the description of murders as great pieces (they are only classed as swivel guns there after) by 1523 (Blackmore, p225), marks the start of the standardisation of naming guns by English ordnance officials.

Slings, demi-slings and quarter slings

Originally a gun of the 'Serpent' class, slings were wrought iron guns fitted to elm stocks with wheels, and were normally given two or three spare chambers. Smaller than port pieces they were considered to be high-velocity, long-range artillery, having a high length to calibre ratio, and were mounted in the waist and the summer and fore castles. Slings fired a shot weighing about 6½lb, had a bore of 5¼in, while the demi-slings and quarter slings fired shot of 3¼lb and had 4 and 3¼in bores respectively. All fired stone, iron and canister shot.

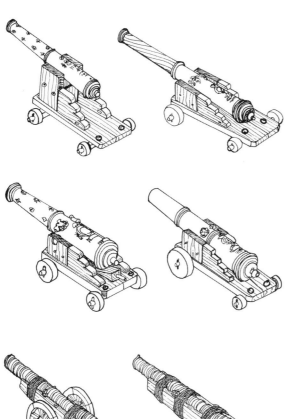

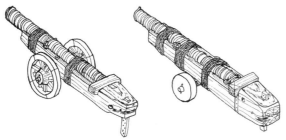

Fig 45 Various types of gun carriages (see also page 112).

The wrought iron gun found on the upper deck, with a bore of 4¼in, may therefore be a 'sling', and the fragments of wrought iron guns with bores just over 3in may be 'quarter slings'.

Fowlers

A form of breech-loading wrought iron gun that fired stone shot. They represent large stocked guns with short barrels, being close quarter low-velocity weapons used against the structure of a vessel. The fowler fired a 6lb shot and had a bore of 5¼in, which would have been effective against the lightly constructed sides of the fore and summercastles and against the crew and soldiers in the waist.

Bases

Bases are small wrought iron swivel guns mounted on minches that slotted into sockets cut into clamps on the inside of the fore and summercastles. They were usually fitted out with three breech chambers and fire a shot ½lb in weight they were up to 3½ft long and had a bore of 2½in.

The thirty 'Bases' may be the swivel guns that were used on yokes pivoted on a wale. One of these was found at the stern, and at least 11 fragments were found in the scour pit below the bow. They had bores between 1½in and 2½in.

Top pieces

Top pieces are thought to be small breech-loading wrought iron swivel guns designed to be used in the ship's fighting tops. These most probably represent short-range guns firing stone shot on a low trajectory.

Cast iron

Cast ordnance was predominately made of brass, though cast iron guns were known. Cast iron guns of an unknown description and size were made in the latter part of Henry V's reign, and might have been large handguns (Rose 1982). Later in Henry VII's reign, cast iron ordnance was certainly made, but would appear to have been weak or too expensive and therefore went out of production. Cast iron guns do not reappear in any quantity (apart from hailshot pieces) until the end of Henry VIII's reign.

Hailshot pieces

Hailshot pieces are short, heavy cast iron handguns with rectangular bores (Fig 46). They are a fire ragged and rough cast iron dice shot. They were a point-blank range defensive weapon and would have been distributed around the ship for defence from boarders. This includes the pavises in the waist, the breast of the summercastle and the barbican or nether deck.

Fig 46 A hailshot piece.

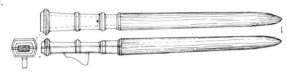

Handguns

The age of the longbow was fast drawing to a close and being replaced by the handgun, a weapon that could fire a 12oz shot on a flat trajectory over 100 yards with enough accuracy to hit a man. Handguns could also be used from within the ship with less space requirements. Furthermore, the effective use of such weapons was not reliant on years of practice, allowing it to become ubiquitous within a short period of time. Henry VIII, between 1544 and 1545, attempted to buy over 10,000 firearms with varying amounts of success (Gairdner and Brodie, p156) and sought to acquire handguns directly through a Milanese merchant, Cristoforo Carcano. By August 1545, 4,200 of the 9,000 harquebuses he ordered had been sent, and at least one of these guns has been found on the ship (Fig 48).

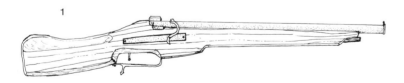

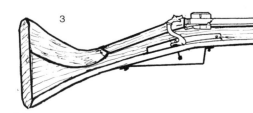

Brass

At the beginning of Henry VIII's reign there were few gun founders capable of casting large and exquisite guns. Henry imported guns from the continent and encouraged Italian gun founders to reside in England. This allowed him to start his own indigenous gun-founding industry as his own subjects learned from their continental equivalents.

Makers

The inscriptions on the cast bronze ordnance (Fig 47) tell us that the cannon were made by R & J Owen in 1535, Peter Bowdus (undated); the demi-cannons by R & J Owen in 1542 and Franciscus Arcanis in 1535 as well as 1542; the culverins made in 1535 (no maker given), Arcanus in 1542 and by Petrus Bowgus in 1543. Furthermore, one of the two demi/bastard culverins was made by R & J Owen in 1537 while the other is unfortunately uninscribed.

Cannon and demi-cannon

Cannon and demi-cannon were the largest of the cast brass guns with the cannon having a bore of 7in and firing a cast iron shot of 45lb. They were probably originally known as curtows. The cannons, weighing 7,000lb, were mounted on elm carriages fitted with truck wheels on the orlop deck and fired out of the lidded gunports. They formed the primary main ship killing armament of the *Mary Rose*.

Fig 47 Ornamentation on cast bronze ordnance.

Fig 48 A selection of handguns: 1 Old German musket 2 Musket from Gordona 3 English musket.

Culverin and demi-culverins

The culverin was a class of cannon with a high length to diameter bore ratio. They were considered guns with a higher velocity and longer range than the cannon. Culverins, 14ft long with a 5 to 5½in bore and 9lb shot came in different sizes and classes, including demi-culverins. By 1545 they were positioned throughout the ship including high up in the barbican of the forecastle and breast of the summercastle providing all round long-range coverage (BL M/485/1–127).

Saker

The smallest of the ordnance class of culverins considered to be effective against ships. The saker had a 4in bore and fired a 3¾in in diameter shot of 5¼lb. Sakers were mounted on elm carriages fitted with trucks in the fore and summercastles. They fired cast iron or stone shot, and, at short-range, canister shot.

Falcon

The second smallest form of the culverin class, Falcons were light cast bronze pieces firing stone, cast iron and lead shot, as well as canister shot of 2½in. The shot weighed 2½lb. They were mounted on small carriages and fitted high up in the fore and summercastles.

Falconets

The smallest of the culverin class, falconets were light cast bronze pieces firing stone, cast iron and lead shot, as well as canister shot of 2¼in and 1 ½lb. They were mounted on small carriages and fitted high up in the fore and summercastles.

Gunpowder

Gunpowder came in two forms, corned and serpentine. Corned powder was in general use while serpentine was finer and used for handguns and priming the touch holes of the guns. The gunpowder was stored in barrels on the lower orlop deck. Before battle it would be poured into cartridges made from paper shaped around formers and then taken to the gun positions. In time of need, the powder could be poured into

Fig 49 Stone shot.

scoops of the correct size and then loaded into the gun.

Shot

The inventories list shot of 'stoen', 'yron' and 'leade' and all three types were found during the excavation of the ship. The stone shot was hewn to varying bore sizes from Kentish ragstone (Fig 49). The iron shot also came in a variety of different sizes and

Fig 50 Iron shot.

some of them had the initial of Henry 'H' on them (Fig 50). While the lead shot was mainly a small shot, there were some with iron dice inside them. The hailshot pieces are noted to fire 'Dyce of yron' or iron dice shot, small squares of iron. Apart from these there were also more exotic types of shot. Between February and April 1513 John Hopton paid a Nicholas Sesse for gunstones '…of iron with crossbars of iron in them…round gunstones of iron' (Knighton and Loades 2003, p20). At the same time 2,700 stone shot were purchased from 'a man of Maidstone'. There were even canister shot, wooden lanterns into which pebbles or the chippings from making stone shot on board could be packed then fired out of any of the guns.

Storage

The shot recovered from the *Mary Rose* has been classed as: 1339 iron, 388 stone, 180 inset, 147 lead, 10 bar, 3 chain, 8 spike and 32 canister shot. Although shot was scattered throughout the ship there were two main concentrations of iron shot on the main deck at either end of the four main guns (M2 and M3 [621 shot] and M6 [249 shot]), while the stone shot was mainly found on the main deck, in sectors M4 and M5 [84 shot] and M6 [123 shot].

Longbows, pikes, bills and darts

So long as boarding remained a primary offensive tactic, weapons to assist or resist it would be required. The weapons carried were the same as used on land, there were no special marine equivalents apart from the Morris pikes (see page 36).

Longbows

The longbow is listed along with its bowstrings and arrows; however, it was at the end of its useful life. Initially used to harry other ships from

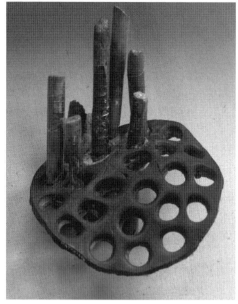

Fig 51 The longbow and a sheave part with surviving arrows.

a distance it still provided a quick and effective weapon at short ranges, where the speed of an accurate archer counted. There are 250 longbows listed supplied in five chests along with 60 gross bowstrings, most probably in barrels. Arrows were supplied in their thousands; 9,600 arrows in total carried in eight chests with 50 sheaves or 192 arrows per chest; a sheave being 24 arrows (Fig 51).

Staff weapons

The *Mary Rose* was supplied with two types of staff weapons, Morris pikes and bills, a hundred of each type. The Morris pike was a shortened version of the full length pike (Fig 54) for use aboard ships; while the bill was a large cleaver-shaped blade combined with vertical and horizontal spikes at the top, fastened to a 6ft-long staff.

Darts

Darts were supplied to be used in the tops (Fig 52), 40 dozen in total most probably supplied in chests. They would be hoisted up prior to battle and thrown down onto the opposing deck to either help repel boarders or to clear the decks before boarding.

Fig 52 A selection of darts.

Personal side arms

The weapons already described were those supplied with the ship, possibly to be used by untrained seamen to help defend the ship in time of need. Apart from these each person could be expected to carry a knife, such as

a bollock dagger for personal defence (Fig 55). Each soldier would have carried a sword (Fig 55) and could be expected to be issued with a leather or chain mail jerkin and even a buckler. The high status officers also might have brought their own favourite weapons, such as gun shields, as illustrated by the excavations of the ship.

Munitions

Munitions represented the tools and certain consumables required to operate the ordnance and artillery. Such tools included crowbars to help train the guns as well as wooden mallets to hammer home the breech wedges and to take them out. Interestingly, during this period there are only powder scoops, rammers and formers listed, the latter to make cartridges. With linstocks (Fig 53) these tools are all that are needed to serve a gun during the Tudor period. Cartridge paper is also noted.

Fig 53 A serpent-headed linstock.

Habiliments of war

This category represents the general stores and spares required during a campaign at sea. All guns would have to have spares. Experimental firing suggests that axles and trucks would have to be replaced on a regular basis, as hinted by the inventories (Hildred *pers. comm.* 2002). Apart from the naval requirements, there were also those of the land army. The ships could be expected to carry stakes and hammers, to provided field defences for the land army. War in the latter medieval period was never as simple a division as that of the army and navy.

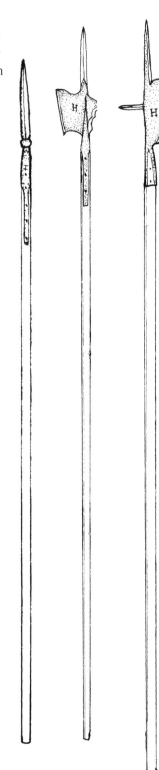

Fig 54 Staff weapons.

Fighting the ship

The *Mary Rose* combined the old with the new, carrying a highly charged superstructure as well as being armed with heavy ordnance. The former was the naval response to the medieval way of waging war through the use of the heavily armed and armoured men-at-arms; while the latter was the seaborne equivalent of the latest siege trains used to breach the defences of castles. As such the *Mary Rose* was a hybrid. She was neither the highly charged medieval ship reliant on her greater size and number of men to win the day, nor was she yet 'the ship of the line' reliant on her weight of shot to beat the enemy into surrender.

From their invention gunpowder and guns were seen on board ships just as soon as they were on land. Throughout the 15th century heavy guns can be found deployed in the waist of ships with lighter guns in the fore and summercastles (Guilmartin 1994, p139–150). Initially they complemented other weapons, such as longbows, javelins, crossbows and darts. They were used to harry the enemy ships from a distance as they manoeuvred to gain advantage before boarding. The smoke and noise from a gun was also considered to cause disruption prior to boarding. As such they were generally seen as a defensive weapon.

During this early period the guns were powerful enough to cause damage, but the confined nature of ships meant they would not have been as potent as they should have been. Space is always at a premium on board a ship, but space was exactly what guns and their gun crews required if they were to be developed as an offensive weapon. Until the more aggressive and offensive tactical use of guns in a stand-off bombardment, designed to reduce the superstructure of ships prior to boarding, was realised space would always be given to extra troops. However, it was quickly realised that seaborne-mounted guns could provide an offensive force.

Fighting tactics

The *Mary Rose* was designed to fight with her guns as the primary offensive weapon. The ship would sail towards the other fleet in an aggressive manner. That would either mean sailing down on another vessel all guns blazing and then grappling and boarding in the time old fashion, charging each other just as two knights would when jousting on land; or for the first time being able to attack the enemy from a distance when they had the upper hand, otherwise termed the weather gauge.

Guns gave a ship the ability to attack another vessel at a distance. Initially this only seemed to favour those in defence, ie those on the leeward side. It is easy to see how this could become an offensive weapon, if you could bring your guns to bear and fire quick enough you could reduce your enemy no matter

if they had the weather gauge or not. Such actions appear to be described during the battle off Brest in the first of Henry's French wars (Spont).

References

Blackmore, HL, *The Armouries of the Tower of London*, Ordnance, 1976

Gairdner, J and Brodie, RH (Ed), *Letters and Papers, Foreign and Domestic, Henry VIII*, Vol 19 Part 2, August–December 1544, 1905

Rose, S, (Ed), *The Navy of the Lancastrian Kings: Accounts and Inventories of William Soper, Keeper of the King's Ships, 1422–1427*, Navy Records Society, Vol 123, 1982

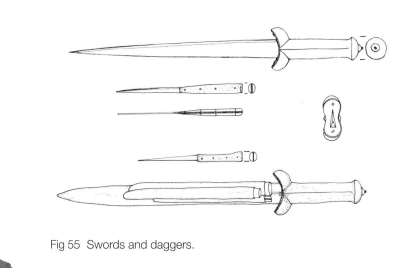

Fig 55 Swords and daggers.

5 MANNING THE MARY ROSE

The crew of the *Mary Rose* consisted of mariners, soldiers, gunners, officers, pilots and surgeons, as well as the master and captain. When the ship served as flagship or vice-flagship of the fleet it also included the 'Lord High Admiral' or a vice-admiral. The servants of the high-ranking officers would also be on board but were not really classed as crew. Throughout the career of the *Mary Rose* the crew size remained just over 400, thus indicating the ship's physical size did not actually change. The crew was divided roughly in half between mariners and soldiers/gunners. Officers, their retinues and specific occupations such as surgeons, musicians and cooks do not appear to be included in the list.

Names

Apart from the senior members of the crew few names are given; however, now and again we are given individual's names. In 1513 we are told Edward Bray was captain of the *Mary Rose*, Rob Symson was the surgeon, John Brerely the purser and an Andrew Fysche is recorded as being a gunner on board. Fysche received a payment of 13s 4d 'to heal him of his hurts'. Another interesting character mentioned was Richard Barker, alias 'Skenthroppe', from London. On 11 June 1539 Skenthroppe and friends were noted as '…Making merry at the said house in Deptford until 10 of the clock in the night, and then departed from the said house and came down to the water's side and called to the *Mary Rose* for the boat.' Unfortunately the ship's boat did not hear them, leading to a comical sequence of events that saw them court martialled. Of interest is that Skenthroppe refers to a facial defect, most probably a squint of some form (Knighton and Loades 2002, p101–104).

Punishment

An insight into the harsh corporal punishment in the Tudor navy can be given by a court-martial held aboard the *Mary Rose* during the First French War 1512–1514. A certain Jacques Berenghier, a merchant from Lille, was forced to join the crew of the *Mary John* as a gunner. He was charged and found guilty of sabotage (Knighton and Loades 2002, p16) by overloading a number of guns, with two stones wrapped in rope, which subsequently burst when fired. He was also noted to be carrying flints and loose gunpowder. After being found guilty he was examined and tortured to discover if he had any accomplices which resulted in him losing a foot. After this he was returned to Sir Edward Howard, the Lord High Admiral, aboard the *Mary Rose* where he was sentenced to have his ears cropped.

Crew lists

The first recorded crew lists of 1513 (CSP I–I, 1661, p750–753) gives the ship between 400 and 402 men. These men are separated between the captain and master, 200 unspecified men under the command of the captain and 200 mariners under the master. From March to April 1513 expenses for the ship's crew include 20 gunners and an additional 20 members of Sir Edward Howard's retinue (Lord High Admiral). The last crew list for 1513, in the naval payments for 4 July to 28 August 1513 (CSP I–II 2305, p1032–1034), lists the ship as having a crew of 402 men.

The crew lists for the following year, 1514, give a total of 350 men (CSP I–II 2652, p1179). However, in the recorded 'Expenses of the war', 25 April 1514, the crew numbers 405. The crew is broken down into 185 soldiers, 200 mariners and 20 gunners (CSP I–II 2842, p1235). A list from later on in the career of the *Mary Rose* (1522–1524), gives a total of 400 men broken down into: 126 soldiers, 244 mariners and 30 gunners. In the same document two surgeons are also referred to as being on board. The last known crew list is that in the Anthony Roll, 1545. This gives a final complement of 415 men, a slight increase over previous years. The crew is broken down into 185 soldiers, 200 mariners and 30 gunners. The crew lists appear to be relatively consistent between 1514 and 1545, but with a slight yet significant increase of 10 men as additional gunners.

Fig 56 Hans Holbein drawing of a typical merchant man and crew c1530.

Dead pays

A term used to describe an accounting procedure used to allow for more money than there were actual men. This meant extra pay for victuals, etc, which was used to supplement those of the officers. In 1513 this would have amounted to 35 men in the *Mary Rose*. This obviously complicates any assessment of the true numbers and division of the crew (Knighton and Loades 2002, p21).

OFFICERS

Lord High Admiral and Vice-Admiral

The position of Lord High Admiral was permanent, while that of vice-admiral was temporary. The description of Lord High Admiral varies. When granted in 1512 to Sir Edward Howard, he was described as 'admiral of England, Ireland and Acquitane' but by 1513 Wales, Normandy and Gascony had also been added to the title. The post of Lord High Admiral was granted to a senior member of the aristocracy, while that of vice-admiral was usually taken up by a lesser member of the aristocracy, quite often only for the duration of a campaign. In 1522 Sir William Fitzwilliam served aboard the *Mary Rose* as vice-admiral during the second French War. He had previously served as captain of the *Mary Rose* (1513) and would later become Lord High Admiral (1536). In July 1545 Sir George Carew was appointed vice-admiral the day before he commanded the *Mary Rose* into battle for the last time. In 1543 John Dudley, otherwise known as Viscount Lisle, was appointed to the office of Lord High Admiral and he held it at the time the *Mary Rose* sank.

Fig 57 William Fitzwilliam 1st Earl of Southampton (c1536–1540).

Captain

The captain of the ship was in overall command of the vessel, her crew and more specifically the soldiers. The position was generally appointed from the

Fig 58 Sir George Carew.

gentry or minor aristocracy. The appointment of captain of the *Mary Rose* was considered a high-profile position. It is no coincidence that several of the captains appointed to the *Mary Rose*, such as Sir William Fitzwilliam and Sir Thomas Wyndham, attained high rank within the navy and socially. Sir Edward Bray was captain of the *Mary Rose* in May 1513, but Sir Henry Sherborne was captain by 1514. The *Mary Rose*'s last captain was Sir George Carew, also vice-admiral of the fleet at the time of her loss.

Master

The captain was the senior serving ship's officer in overall charge of the vessel. However, the master was in charge of the sailing of the ship. As such the master was a professional seaman, who need not have been selected from the gentry or aristocracy, though they probably came from families of some wealth. John Clerke commanded the *Mary Rose* on her first open water transit from Portsmouth to the Thames; however, Thomas Sperte was the first true master of the *Mary Rose,* commanding her from October 1511. Sperte was a remarkable man who had the confidence of the King. He later became the master of the *Henry Grace à Dieu*, a yeoman of the crown and in 1517 he commanded an exploring expedition (Oppenheim 1896b, p91) and from 10 November 1514 by letters patent he enjoyed an annuity of £20 a year. Then he handed over command of his ship, most probably to John Browne, who is first mentioned as master of the *Mary Rose* in a warrant of 2 March 1514, and who still held the position in 1522.

Pilots

The *Mary Rose* carried pilots, sometimes known as lodesmen, to help the master navigate in unfamiliar waters. Pilots were professional seamen and navigators. Some were employed for their local knowledge around harbours, while others were employed to actually navigate the vessel on voyages. We know that a John Wodlas conducted the *Mary Rose* through the North Sea (Knighton and Loades 2002, p64).

CREW

Senior crew

Assisting the officers in the running of the ship were a boatswain, a master's mate, purser and quartermaster. Tradesmen carried on board probably consisted of carpenters, stewards and cooks. The senior officers also took aboard members of their own retinue. These craftsmen and junior officers were paid at least twice as much as an ordinary seaman.

Mariners

At least half of the crew were classed as mariners. The core of these men would have been professional seamen drawn from the coastal towns and villages, or even other countries like Spain or France. Landsmen driven to a career at sea by poverty or famine would have made up numbers.

Soldiers and gun crews

The vast majority of soldiers on board, as on land, came from the county militia. Military training would have been provided at the musters and longbow training at the butts. It is known that men from the militia of Oxfordshire were appointed 'to go to sea' with Sir George Carew, and therefore probably drowned on the vessel when it sank (Acts of the Privy Council). It is most probable that the soldiers formed, under the guidance of the gun captains, the gun crews.

Master gunner

The master gunner was in overall charge of gun crews and guns. He would have stood station on the poop deck with the other senior officers, being available for discussions on tactics and strategy.

Gun captains

The gunners in the crew lists were the gun captains. They directed those in the gun crew made up of either mariners or soldiers. There would have been one gun captain per heavy gun, these being slings/sakers or bigger.

Servants

All high-ranking officers could be expected to bring servants with them. In 1513 Admiral Howard had 31 servants on board and his captain a further 16 (Knighton and Loades 2002, p12). An allowance would also have to be made for victualling the servants.

References

Acts of the Privy Council 1542–7, 188, 571
CSP I–I, 1661, p750–753
CSP I–II, 2305, p1032–1034
CSP I–II, 2652, p1179
CSP I–II, 2842, p1235

Fig 59 One of several animal skeletons found – one of the ship's dogs.

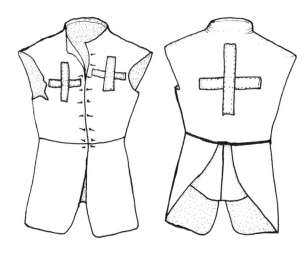

Fig 60 Leather jerkin with St George's Cross of the sort worn by a soldier.

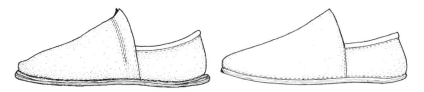

Fig 61 Shoes.

6 LIFE ON BOARD THE MARY ROSE

The *Mary Rose* as a sailing man-of-war carried soldiers and gunners to fight, and sailors to sail. These men with their food, beer and water, as well as an area to prepare the food, spares to fix broken rigging and armaments plus enough space to allow them room to sleep and rest, had to be accommodated in the ship. The whole ship was separated into sectors based around the natural division of the riders, deck beams, standing knees and the partitioning between them.

The ship's layout

The *Mary Rose* is divided vertically into decks with each deck split into a defined area by athwartship partitioning forming bulkheads. They were made from horizontally laid planks nailed to stanchions and partition supports. Some of the partitions also have sliding doors and formed cabins in discreet areas.

The lowest part of the ship was the hold which was formed by the deck above (the lower orlop). The bottom of the hold was covered by ballast shingle. In the centre of the hold was the mainmast sitting in its mast step. On the port side of the mast was the pump, surrounded by partitioning to keep the pump clear of obstructions. The hold was divided into three areas, the aft lantern store, the main food store and forward of the mast step the kitchen. The kitchen consisted of two large brick ovens with copper cauldrons. Forward of this was the fuel store where the birch logs for the oven were kept. Just forward of this a ladder, which stretched from the hold to the main orlop, allowed the crew access to the decks above.

The lower orlop or false orlop extended the full length of the ship and was divided into eight areas. The forward two sectors represented a store for rigging and spares needed for gun carriages. Just aft of this appears to be where the gunpowder, pitch and tar were kept. The dangerous lanterns with their tallow candles were kept well away at the other end of the orlop deck, where they could only be accessed from the deck above. The area in front of the lantern store was the purser's cabin, where personal items were kept safe. Forward of this was the weapons store, where crates of longbows and arrows along with personal chests could be found. Further casks full of beer were stored here as well. The orlop deck above the galley formed the smoke hood and on either side was the anchor cable store.

The orlop or main orlop was the first covered and waterproof deck, and was being caulked along its full length, with waterways cut in the standing knees to allow water to run to the scuppers along the central part of the hull. The orlop is dominated by the heavy guns, interspersed in the aft part by cabins, that of the barber surgeon, the ship's carpenter, bosun and master rigger. In the forwards part of the orlop were a few cabins for the junior officers, who had the privilege of a separate cabin where they could practise their navigation in peace. Access to the decks above was via a pair of companionways at either end of the waist.

The upper deck is divided into three parts; the nether deck below the forecastle, the waist open to the elements, and the nether deck below the summercastle. The nether deck below the forecastle housed the anchor handling area. Here was sited the hawser holes where the anchor cables came into the ship, took a turn around the bitts and the capstan under the forecastle, then lead aft and down into the lower orlop. Aft of this was the waist. Here four wrought iron breech-loading slings were arranged along either side, firing over the gunwale but behind a screen of pavises. This was also an area where archers could harry the opposing ship and soldiers would muster before boarding. In the centre of the ship the sheet anchor was stored, its cable running forward and the anchor itself aft. The aft part of the waist was predominated by the mainmast and its rigging. The nether deck below the summer deck was an area set aside for handling the rigging

Fig 62 Reconstruction of the kitchen.

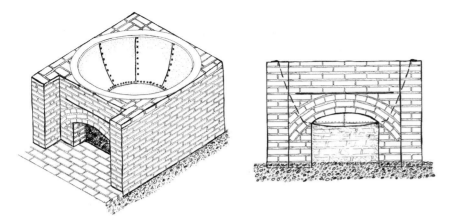

Fig 63 A brick oven.

where the officers lived, played and ate. The Great Cabin was situated here and, as Bourne tells us:
'The master-gunner, like the master and pilot, messed in the Great Cabin, and the carpenter was a key man, responsible for the fabric of the ship.' (Bourne 1963, p12).

It would have been in these upper parts of the summercastle that Sir George Carew and possibly even Henry VIII himself would have dined, and slept.

Victualling

Evidence for food aboard the *Mary Rose* comes from the accounts of victuals carried and the remains of food found during the excavation (Gardiner 2006). The cost of victualling a crew was worked out at a daily, weekly or monthly rate per head of men on board. In 1512 this amounted to 5 shillings a month per man (Spont). This remained unchanged until 1520.

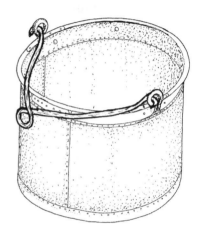

Fig 66 Copper Kettle.

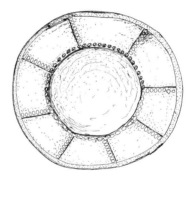

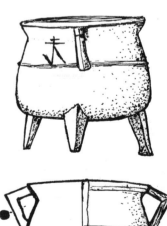

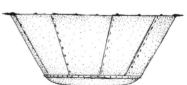

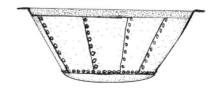

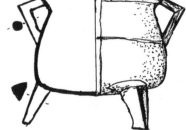

Fig 64 Reconstruction of kitchen with both ovens and their smoke hood.

as well as by 1545 the mounting of a number of heavy guns. It acted as a muster point and was where the majority of soldiers would be when not at action stations. It is where the tiller came through the transom and the ship was steered.

In the bows above the nether deck was the forecastle. This consisted of two full decks surmounted by an open half deck. The lowest deck was equipped to help handle the anchors. The rest of the forecastle was given over to soldiers and gunners. It was a fighting platform. The summercastle and deck above was also primarily a fighting platform, but just as importantly was

Fig 65 Dish for use in the oven.   Fig 67 Copper cauldron.

Higher agricultural prices had an impact and by 1522 the rate increased to 18 pence a week or 6 shillings a month. By 1545 this had risen to 8 shillings per head per month. The officers and Admiral supplemented their own rations from their personal income. Although the prices changed, the staple diet of the crew did not. The early Tudor seaman was provided with bread, biscuit, salt beef, fish, cheese, butter and beer.

Biscuit was a kind of crisp dry bread prepared flat and double baked ('bis cocus') so it was more or less hard. It was made from flour and water or milk without leaven. The *Regent*'s victualling accounts in 1512 show that 3,000lb of 'biscuite' was purchased at a cost of 100 shillings. This was expected to feed 300 mariners for 10 days, making 1lb of biscuit per day per man. The advantage hard-baked biscuit had over bread was that it could be stored for a greater length of time.

Beer was issued for the same reason as opposed to water, which would go stale. It was issued at 1 gallon per man per day, though was obviously not as strong as modern-day equivalents. In 1522 140 pipes of beer were considered sufficient for 200 men for eight weeks. This was a rate of one pipe per day for every 120 men. This was increased in 1545, when one pipe was issued for every 100 men.

Salt beef was the main form of meat issued and it was eaten on certain days. It was done at a rate of one pipe per 100 men per week, a pipe in 1522 containing 2½ oxen. Furthermore by February 1545 eight tons of flesh (beef) contained 800 pieces of beef, and was estimated to serve four days in the week for 2,000 men for eight weeks. This made one piece

of beef per man for the four 'meat' days in the week. It is estimated that a hogshead held about 500lb of meat, making the daily ration 2½lbs per 'meat day'.

The remaining three days of the week were 'fish days'. The fish was generally 'stock fische', 'sawlte fysche' (salt fish), 'western fisshe' or 'drye hake'. The main types of fish would appear to have been cod, hake, ling and conger. There were two types of ways to cure the fish, either salting or splitting them and air drying them, otherwise known by the generic term stock fish. In 1522 18,000 salt fish were required to feed 3,000 men for eight weeks (Brewer). This would be one piece per day for every four men on the three non-meat days. It is possible that fish was not served on all three days or that freshly caught fish supplemented the stock or salt fish. Cheese and butter formed welcome additions to the weekly rations.

Apart from the main victual, other things were bought for the crew including: mustard seeds, oil, vinegar and fats. These no doubt were used for

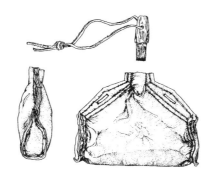

Fig 68 Wooden spoon and turned wooden bowls.

Fig 69 Leather water bottle.

Fig 70 Tankards, bowls and dishes.

the officers and barber surgeon for medicinal purposes, but could also have been used to supplement the crew's basic rations. To gain an understanding of what else the officers and admirals might request we can use Lord Howard's stores from the late 15th century. The extra stores loaded on board his ship included: '...mutton, pork, calve, salmon, weys, oatmeal, green and grey peas and eggs'.

Lord Howard's private supplies included: '...a panyer with spices, halfe abarel resons corans, the almonds and the rys, the lampreys and the sturgeon, the mustard seede...'. It also included '3 bates Malmesey', a 'hoggeghead of white wyn' [white wine], a 'pipe white wyn of schore', a 'pipe white wyn of albon...'. Further to this '...freshe watter fysche...' such as 'carpe', 'breme', 'ellis', and salt water fish such as 'playseys', 'wyttynges', 'whelkes', 'solys', 'codddys hede', 'moscollys', 'zerbys', 'pekerellys', 'grene fysche', 'whyght heryng', 'kokyllis', 'oysters' and 'shyrympis'. Other ingredients included: 'oylle', 'synamen', 'spyssys', 'allmendys', 'mustard' and 'vinegar'. Such variation in supplies were beyond the means of the common seaman.

References

Bourne, W, *A Regiment for the Sea and other Writings on Navigation by William Bourne of Gravesend, a Gunner, (c1535–1582)*, Cambridge University Press, 1963

Brewer, JS, *Letters and Papers, Foreign and Domestic, Henry VIII*, Vol 3, 1519–1523, 1867

Gardiner, J and Allen, MJ (Ed), *Before the mast: life and death aboard the Mary Rose*, The Archaeology of the Mary Rose Vol 4, Mary Rose Trust, 2005

Fig 72 Personal items.

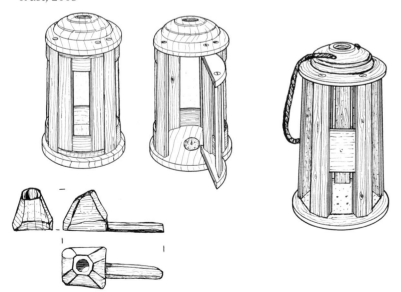

Fig 71 Lanterns and candle holder.

Fig 73 Stools and jugs.

Navigation equipment on board the *Mary Rose*

The *Mary Rose* has shone new light onto the sophisticated nature of navigation in the Tudor world. Though sailing at a time when Magellan had circumnavigated the world and Cabot had found the 'New found land' in North America, most historians considered English navigation during the 1540s as only suitable for rudimentary coasting. The navigational instruments found on the *Mary Rose* would have allowed it to sail beyond sight of land and the coast in heaving seas, and arrived at the destination port on the right tide. They allowed the *Mary Rose* to sail with confidence out into the North Sea beyond sight of land to arrive in Scotland at an agreed port. The *Mary Rose* also sailed south towards Brest in the northern part of the Bay of Biscay; a route that would have allowed her to feel the North Atlantic swell under her keel.

The navigational instruments were quite sophisticated. The binnacle compass with lead weight added to its bottom, would have stayed upright and ensured the compass needle kept pointing north, no matter how much the ship moved. The sand glasses kept time, allowing the mariner to plot course run and time run. The log line would have given an estimate of speed through the water and therefore a rough estimate of distance run. A pair of traditional one-hand brass navigation dividers allowed the navigator to mark out course run with one hand while steadying the chart and himself with his other hand. Sounding leads gave the depth of water below the keel, and armed with tallow would read the type of seabed. It also alerted the mariner to the shallows of land approaching. The tide gauge then ensured that the navigator could arrive on the correct tide at the destination port.

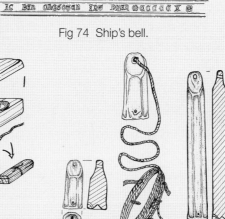

Fig 75 Sand glass.

Fig 74 Ship's bell.

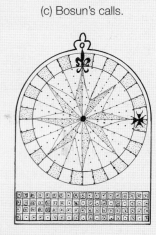

(a)

(b)

(c)

Fig 76 (a) Captain's, (b) Master's and (c) Bosun's calls.

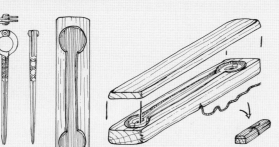

Fig 77 Dividers and case.

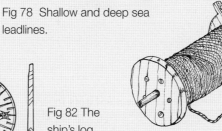

Fig 78 Shallow and deep sea leadlines.

Fig 79 Travis board.

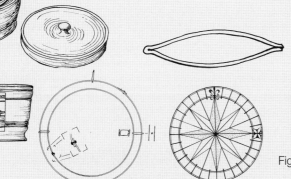

Fig 80 The ship's compass.

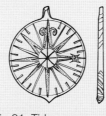

Fig 81 Tide gauge.

Fig 82 The ship's log.

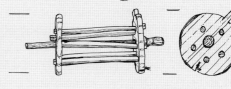

7 SEAMANSHIP AND SHIP HANDLING

The *Mary Rose* was built as a fighting platform, but more importantly the ship had to operate first as a sailing ship. Therefore space had to be available to operate the rigging and sails, and when needs be the anchors. Anchor handling was an important part of operating the ship at sea, especially in such strong tidal areas as the south coast of England.

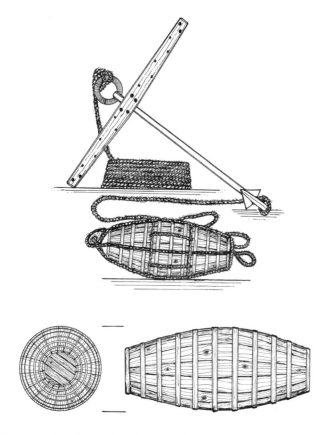

Fig 83 Bower anchor, line and anchor buoy (see also page 107).

Sailing descriptions

The *Mary Rose* was considered by contemporary commentators to be a good sailor. Throughout her career we have documents that refer to her sailing capabilities. During Tudor times certain terms were used to describe sailing techniques. When sailing into the wind, termed 'on a wind' certain extremes are described such as 'on a bowline', which meant sailing into the wind, while with 'a bowline inboard' or 'tack aboard' meant hard on the wind. Sailing downwind was classed as 'sheets let fly', and on a broad reach was termed 'slackening'. Despite being considered a good sailor, the *Mary*

Rose was still reliant on favourable winds to be able to set sail on the course she wished.

A typical set of events is described during the summer of 1522. Fitzwilliam recorded the sailing qualities of his fleet during unfavourable weather. In a letter to the King he tells him that the *Henry Grace à Dieu* sailed better than any other ship in the fleet. She weathered all the ships in the fleet save the *Mary Rose*, there being nothing between them when sailing 'on a wind'. On the 21 June Fitzwilliam wrote to the King from aboard the *Mary Rose*, stating that he doubted '…much more of the victual than wind…' meaning he was more worried about victuals than he was about the strong wind. Due to damage sustained to the *Henry Grace à Dieu*, her victuals were unloaded and distributed to the rest of the fleet, allowing the fleet to sail for Dartmouth. On 23 June it was off St Helens, at the east end of the Isle of Wight, sailing westward on a broad reach with a light northerly wind. However, unfortunately due to contrary winds it had only reached Portland by 27 June. The wind then backed round to the east or north-east

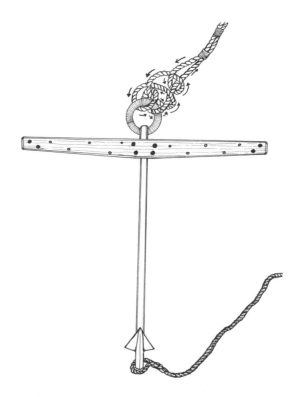

Fig 84 Anchor – stocked with anchor cable tied to the anchor ring and anchor trip spliced to the crown (see also page 107).

allowing the fleet to get underway again and it reached Dartmouth on the evening of 29 June. At Dartmouth they collected water on 30 June, after which the *Mary Rose* led the fleet across the Channel to France where three days later Surrey wrote to Wolsey stating that he had taken the French port of Morlaix.

Plying the tides

Sailing ships of this period were at the beck and call of the wind, weather and tides. When the wind was not blowing from a favourable direction then the tides could be used to help transport a ship along the coast. The ship would anchor when the tide was running against the direction of travel then raise the anchors when running in the required direction allowing the ship to be carried along on the tide. This was called 'plying the tides'. A ship could also 'warp' or 'kedge' her way out of a port, by laying her anchors out before it and hauling in on the anchor cable. In this way the ship could cover short distances, such as out of harbour into the open sea.

During the same fleet manoeuvres (1522) as discussed previously we get an idea as to the importance of the anchors. On 30 May 1522 the *Mary Rose* was at Dover waiting to set sail westward to Southampton. The wind was north to easterly when Vice-Admiral Fitzwilliam noted it increased and changed to west-south-west. The wind blew so hard that the Admiral ordered his fleet to sail eastwards. When they reached the Downs the fleet anchored there until 2 June until the wind changed to west-by-north allowing it to continue westwards to Southampton by plying the tides. This meant anchoring during the flood when the tide was flowing east, then drifting west with ebb tide. Unfortunately, as soon as the wind went back to the south-west the fleet had to put back to the Downs, where they were still at anchor on 4 June. The Admiral noted the characteristics of both the *Mary Rose* and *Henry Grace à Dieu* while at anchor, stating that when the wind blew 'sore and strainably' all day on 3 June, the *Henry Grace à Dieu* rode as still and gentle at anchor as the best ship in the fleet. Despite this she seems to have lost her fore topmast and main topmast as well as her bowsprit, having to make for Portsmouth for repairs.

Fig 85 A recovered anchor with cable behind it.

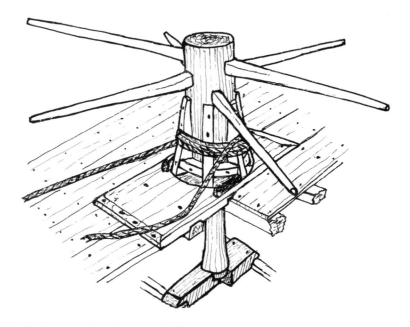

Fig 86 Capstan (see also page 108).

47

8 THE HISTORY OF THE MARY ROSE

The *Mary Rose* was completed in the summer of 1511 and lay on the Thames as political events unfolded. A year later the *Mary Rose* was involved in her first war, the first of three against the French. As a ship the *Mary Rose* had a long and colourful career (Fig 87); however, much of it was to be in ordinary, lying up in the Thames (Fig 88).

First French War, 1512–1514

In April 1512 Sir Edward Howard was appointed Lord High Admiral, taking the newly completed *Mary Rose* as his flagship, rather than the older but much larger *Regent*. This was a significant decision by a man now 35 years old, with a wealth of experience having been knighted while serving in Scotland in 1497 when only 20 years old. It is a strong vote of confidence in the perceived capabilities of the newer but smaller *Mary Rose*. Thomas Sperte was to be the master of the *Mary Rose*. Sir Thomas Wyndham, who died in 1521, was also based on the *Mary Rose*.

Howard's duties were set out in a document dated 8 April 1512. His fleet carried between 5,000 and 6,000 men in 18 ships, the largest of which were the *Regent* (1,000 tons), the *Mary Rose* (500 tons), and the *Peter Pomegranate* (400 tons). The latter two though, at least half the size of the *Regent*, carried a more powerful armament of ordnance than it. Howard was to sweep the English Channel clear of the enemy. He was to be at sea

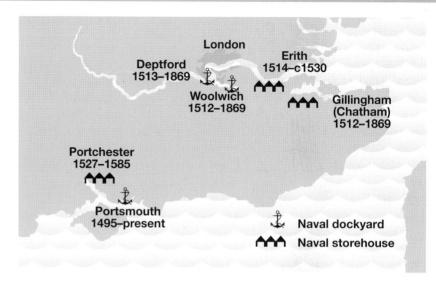

Fig 88 The main shore establishments of Henry VIII, with which the *Mary Rose* would have been familiar with.

for the next three months, clearing the sea of French naval opposition between England and northern Spain before returning to Southampton. These operations allowed for the safe passage of a second fleet, carrying an English army of 10,000 to 12,000 men, to Fuenterrabía on the north-east coast of Spain, close to the French border.

Howard's fleet set sail in April for a three-month cruise, during which time Howard had taken at least 12 Breton and French ships, and followed this up by landing soldiers in Brittany. Over four days the soldiers won several battles, captured many knights and other gentlemen, and burned the towns and villages for 30 miles around, among which was Conquet. Sir Edward Howard's fleet returned to Southampton in June to plan the next stages of the offensive against France. Howard met the King at Southampton on 1 July (Matthew and Harrison, p335–337).

The Battle of Brest

On 10 August 1512, in high winds and heavy seas, Howard put to sea again. The Venetian Envoy in England tells us:

'Towards 11am, off Brest, the lookout man of the Admiral's galley discovered some two leagues off in the mouth of the Gulf of Brest a number of ships, which proved to be the French fleet. Chase given with extreme joy by the Admiral in his ship of 500 tons [the *Mary Rose*] and another of 400 [the *Peter Pomegranate*], commanded by a valiant knight, called Sir Anthony

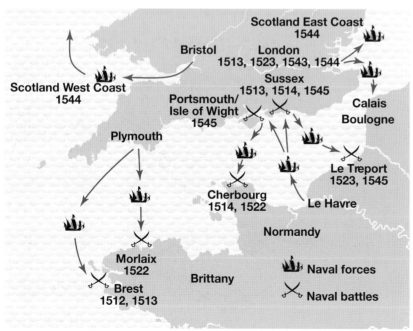

Fig 87 The main operations and battles at sea between 1512 and 1546.

Fig 89 The *Regent* and the *Queen* grappled together and burning during the battle of Brest.

Ughtred, they leaving the other ships a quarter of a league astern, lest the French, who were in force at anchor and so near shore, should sheer off, as they, however, did. The English Admiral cannoned the French Admiral, compelled him to cut his cables, and put to sea, and with a single shot from a heavy bombard disabled his mast, and killed 300 men, the ship saving itself among the rocks. Attack in the meanwhile by the ship of 400 tons on the carrack of Brest, called the *Queen*, of 400 tons burden, and carrying 400 men. The former did not grapple, but in a moment riddled the latter so between wind and water by shots from six large 'cortos', that the French could not keep her afloat. With the rest of the English fleet arriving, the *Regent* of 800 tons boarded the carrack with 400 men. She surrendered but the powder magazine (containing 300 barrels for the use of the French fleet) blew up instantly. The explosion was so furious that the *Regent* caught fire and both ships were burned together. At least 180 of the *Regent*'s men threw themselves into the sea and were saved by the ships' boats of the English fleet. Of the French, only six escaped, and they were made prisoners. The ship of Sir Anthony Ughtred, with 30 men, sheered off, and during two days the whole of the English fleet remained in this bay of Brest to raise the anchors of the 53 French ships.'

Nearly all the men were lost, including the captain and Howard's brother-in-law Sir Thomas Knevet, Sir John Carew and all the 600 soldiers and sailors. On the French side, casualties were also high and included Mons de Clermont, High Admiral of France and the seneschal of the town of Morlaix.

Unperturbed by this loss, the next day the English landed soldiers ashore, captured 800 people in the process and burned 'many places on land'. They also burned 27 French ships and captured five more. Unfortunately stormy weather forced the English fleet to return home to Dartmouth. A number of the ships were separated partly due to storm damage. These ships headed to Southampton for repairs. By 14 October the *Mary Rose* was one of several warships moored at Southampton. The King meet his ships' masters, including Thomas Sperte of the *Mary Rose*, at Eltham Palace in north Kent. During the meeting they decided it was too late in the season for more action and that the fleet should winter in the Thames, not far from Eltham.

At the start of 1513 the *Mary Rose* was still moored in the Thames and the opportunity was taken to repair her guns while the King and his advisors considered the manning requirements of the navy. Towards the start of spring, the fleet was prepared for the forthcoming fighting season. Sir Edward Howard was reaffirmed as Admiral and chose the *Mary Rose* as his flagship. He appointed himself as captain in command of the 200 soldiers on board while Thomas Sperte continued as the ship's master with 200 mariners. For the first time we are told that a Mr Davison commanded the *Mary Rose*'s tender, described as a bark. We are also told that *The Baptist of Harwich* was assigned to the *Mary Rose* to supply victuals.

The movements of the fleet are set out in the *Mary Rose*'s expenses between 14 March and 16 July 1513. On 18 March the *Mary Rose* lay at anchor at Woolwich. From here Howard wrote to Wolsey expressing concerns about the victuals of the fleet. He also advised that a person captured from the *Marya de Loretta* should 'be well twitched, for I ween he can speak news'. The next morning, Saturday 19 March, the King visited the fleet, after which it set sail down the Lower Thames on the ebb tide.

Brittany

The fleet set sail for Brittany from the Thames via Plymouth. Henry had decided to use his fleet to transport his army under the command of Charles Brandon, Lord Lisle, to attack Brittany. After leaving the Thames, Howard infamously raced the fleet off north-east Kent (see seaman and seamanship on page 46). He ended his letter describing the race still requesting much-needed victuals. Fourteen days later, by the 5 April, the fleet was moored off Plymouth and in desperate need of victuals. The *Mary Rose* had victuals for 15 days while the *Katharine Fortileza* had none. Howard knew there were plenty of victuals at Sandwich, but refused to leave Plymouth, thinking the enemy fleet was approaching Devon. The

Fig 90 Henry VIII.

Fig 91 The siege of Boulogne. A Cowdry sketch showing Henry's fleet on the far right supporting his troops.

shortage of victuals was to remain a problem when the fleet sailed from Plymouth on Sunday 10 April. A strong north-north-east wind took it across to Brest, arriving there the next day. At Brest the French fleet consisted of 15 vessels lying in the outer harbour. On seeing the English fleet they retreated into the safety of the inner harbour, where they joined 50 more ships under the defences of the castle. Previously the French King, Louis, had ordered his Admiral, Pregent de Bidoux, to bring his galleys around from the Mediterranean to Brittany and Brest.

Unable to engage the French directly, Howard landed men onshore close to Brest. They managed to burn some houses before being opposed by 10,000 French. The French blockaded the harbour by mooring hulks across the entrance. Howard considered landing men with a gun to sink the hulks but instead launched an attack by sea on Friday 22 April. In the ensuing battle the French galleys sank 'Master Compton's ship' and crippled a new barque. To try and negate the threat of the galleys, Howard led an attack against them in four shallow-draught boats on Tuesday 25 April. Despite the French vessels being heavily defended by guns and crossbows Howard managed to board the galley of Admiral Bidoux with 17 men securing a

cable, to its capstan. The French severed the cable, leaving Howard stranded and on the galley. Howard was last seen calling out to his men 'Come aboard again!', 'Come aboard again!', before being attacked by armed men and 'cast overboard with morris pikes'. Admiral Bidoux managed to recover Howard's body with his admiral's badge of office and a bosun's call. This was given to the French Queen while his armour was given to Madame Claud, the King's daughter. Howard's body was to be 'embalmed' and await the orders of the French King.

On hearing the news of the loss of the Admiral, the English fleet abandoned Brest and returned to Plymouth. News of Howard's death was sent to Henry. On hearing the news, Henry appointed Lord Thomas Howard, elder brother of Sir Edward, as fleet commander. After riding with urgency to Plymouth, Lord Howard took up quarters on the *Mary Rose* on 7 May. Howard immediately assembled the captains of the fleet to carry out a post-mortem on the blockade of Brest. The reasons given for the abandonment of the blockade were a shortage of victuals, the continued threat of the French galleys and that had the wind turned to the west the fleet would have been caught on a lee shore and possibly wrecked. In concluding the post-mortem

Lord Thomas Howard stated that his brother's operation 'was the most dangerous enterprise' he had heard of.

Supporting land operations

On 13 May 1513 Henry wrote to Lord Howard and Sir Charles Brandon (now Lord Lisle) setting out plans for his forthcoming invasion of France. The fleet, under the command of Howard, was to blockade Brest again to 'distress' the French navy now in Brittany. Lord Lisle would join the Admiral at Southampton or Plymouth and command the land forces. The two men were to work closely together.

By 5 June, Howard and the fleet had arrived at Southampton. Here the fleet was loaded with supplies for the attack on France. At this time some of the men took the opportunity to desert. A few of them were captured and held at Hereford Gaol. Henry commanded some of the deserters should be executed as a warning to others. By 14 June the fleet was waiting to get underway again. Howard, having taken station off Quarr Abbey on the north-east coast of the Isle of Wight, wrote to Wolsey and others from the *Mary Rose* stating that '…we are here strong enough to encounter the whole fleet of France, and, had the wind served, had been gone towards Brest ere now'. It would

appear that the wind was never favourable again, though this would be a blessing in disguise as other political events overtook the planned attack on Brest. The *Mary Rose* was soon to see service off the north-east coast of England and play its part in one of the greatest victories of Henry's reign.

Scotland and the north of England

As Howard fretted about contrary winds and victuals, Henry, with his favourite Charles Brandon, set about making plans to invade the north of France. This would be done in alliance with the elderly Emperor Maximilian. Howard moved his fleet to Sandwich to help screen the forthcoming crossing of the army to Calais. The army started its crossing on 6 June with Henry following on 30 June.

In 1513 King James IV of Scotland formed an alliance with France and issued an ultimatum to Henry. On news of Henry's invasion of France, James demanded that Henry withdraw his army from France. Henry ignored this demand and the Scots invaded England. Lord Howard, supported by his sons, including Sir Thomas, defeated a larger Scottish army at the Battle of Flodden on 9 September 1513, killing the Scottish king in the process. The English army was supported by a fleet of 15 ships, including the *Mary Rose,* with Edward Bray as captain. The fleet moved from the south coast to the north and lay at Hull for four days '…afore they landed at Newcastell…' landed troops and ordnance and headed '…toward the Scottish field'. It was Admiral Howard leading the Van with his men, no doubt including those serving him on the *Mary Rose*, which proved the decisive element in the victory at Flodden. After the Battle of Flodden and Henry's less significant campaign in France, the navy was stood down. The *Mary Rose* most probably wintered in the Thames along with the rest of the fleet.

In preparation of the next year's campaigning season, the fleet was assembled and prepared in the Thames. A list of 'The names of the ships, captains, mariners, soldiers and gunners, which be appointed to be in the King's army by the sea this next year' tells us a John Brown was appointed to be master of the *Mary Rose* and John Brereley purser. In 1514 the *Mary Rose* saw active service between April and 19 June. Sir Henry Sherburn was captain of her 185 soldiers while John Brown commanded the ship and its 200 mariners and 20 gunners. Again the plan was to take the fight to the French, this time by attacking the French galleys commanded by 'Prior John' near Cherbourg. The *Mary Rose* never left the English coast, the main fighting being done by the smaller ships of the fleet. In May, John Wodlas, from Harwich, conveyed the *Mary Rose* from Harwich, to meet the King returning from Calais, possibly after Henry had captured Therouanne and Tournai. After meeting they continued up the Thames to Blackwall. The war was ended in August of that year and the navy was stood down, including the huge and newly launched *Henry Grace à Dieu,* a replacement for the lost *Regent*.

In ordinary c1514–1522

From July 27 1514, the *Mary Rose* was laid up in ordinary at Blackwall on the River Thames, along with the *Peter Pomegranate* and the *Great Elizabeth*. As part of the process of being mothballed in ordinary an inventory was made of all fittings removed from the *Mary Rose*. The anchors, cables, the ship's two boats and their masts and fittings were delivered to John Hopton, comptroller of the King's ships. The bows, arrows, armour, gunpowder, pikes etc, were delivered to John Millet and Thomas Elderton. The guns, shot, flags and a few cooking utensils were to be left aboard the ship in the custody of John Browne and John Bryarley, the master and purser. Between late 1514 and early 1522 the *Mary Rose* remained in this state, though it is likely that at some stage the guns were offloaded to the safety of the Tower.

With no wars planned, the fleet was to be left in ordinary for the next few years. A skeleton crew of four men under the charge of William Mewe lived aboard the vessel between 1517 and 1521. These men helped to look after the ship and stop squatters from using the hull. They would also keep a watch on the ship and report any damages or maintenance requirements. Such general maintenance included recaulking the ship and the need to pump her dry for a day and a night. At such times extra men were recruited to assist the skeleton crew.

Field of the Cloth of Gold

In 1520 the *Mary Rose* took part in an important occasion with several other warships. In June the *Mary Rose* scoured the seas to guard the passage of Henry across the Channel to France to meet Francis I. This meeting of the English and French kings was grandly named 'The Field of the Cloth of Gold'. The aim of the meeting was to find a solution to their differences and so stop any further wars. A peace was agreed, which lasted two years before they were at war again.

Second French War, 1522

In 1522 war was again declared between England and France. Henry had signed a secret treaty with the new Holy Roman Emperor, Charles V. The initial plan was to take Paris, with the English army commanded by Suffolk attacking from Calais in the north and Spanish troops from the south in a double pincer move. In support of the army, the *Mary Rose* with the English navy were to protect the convoys to Calais.

On 30 May 1522, the *Mary Rose* was at Dover. As the flagship of Vice-Admiral Fitzwilliam she was present and probably received the King when he visited the port. The fleet spent the month attempting to get out of the Downs (see page 46) but contrary weather saw them dodge around the Downs for at least a week or so. The *Mary Rose* was still at anchor in the Downs on 4 June 1522, though within a few weeks she was in the Solent.

Once there the fleet embarked an army of 5,000 men. On 19 June Thomas Howard, now Earl of Surrey as a reward for his endeavours at Flodden Field, joined the *Mary Rose,* where he noted the usual problems with victuals. The fleet was supplied with meat, fish and biscuit for two months, but only had beer for one month, while some of the ships were only victualled for eight days. Howard put the problem down to negligence. On 21 June Howard wrote to the King from aboard the *Mary Rose*, stating he doubted '…much more of the victual than wind'.

Despite the shortage of victuals, the fleet set sail for Dartmouth. On 23 June the fleet was off St Helens, at the east end of the Isle of Wight, sailing westward with a light north wind. Due to contrary winds the fleet only reached Portland by 27 June and did not arrive at Dartmouth until the evening of 29 June, where they were able to collect water. A day later on 30 June the *Mary Rose* led the fleet to France. Three days later Howard, writing to Wolsey, stated he had taken the French port of Morlaix. By this time the fleet was in desperate need of victuals with many of Fitzwilliam's ships not having any meat or fish. Howard, now himself on the *Mary Rose,* had beer for 12 days and was having to consider using water! A month later the fleet was back at home and on 3 August Howard left for Calais leaving his Vice-Admiral Fitzwilliam in charge on the *Mary Rose.*

Fig 92 A detail from the painting of the embarkation from Dover showing the coastal forts similar to Southsea Castle firing guns.

Fig 93 The embarkation from Dover.

The campaigning season was coming to an end. Fitzwilliam wrote to Wolsey stating that the *Mary Rose* and *Peter Pomegranate* could be laid up, as no more Great Ships would be wanted unless the French King prepared an army. Fitzwilliam discussed the mothballing of the fleet with the rest of the ships' masters, including John Browne of the *Mary Rose* and John Clogge of the *Peter Pomegranate*. The discussions included where to berth the *Henry Grace à Dieu* and the King's other Great Ships for the winter. The deliberations included making soundings in the Camber off Rye to find a suitable place for the fleet. As no other place suitable for the King's ships could be found, all the masters agreed that Portsmouth and Dartmouth were the best places. On 30 June, Thomas Howard recommended to Henry VIII that the fleet winter in the well-protected haven of Dartmouth. For the rest of the war, until 1525, the *Mary Rose* did not see any further active service. Instead she was held in reserve along with 10 other warships moored in Portsmouth Harbour.

In ordinary, 1522–1539

After the war the fleet was dispersed. The *Henry Grace à Dieu* was moored at Northfleet, the *Gabriel Royal* was moored off Erith, the *Sovereign* lay in a dock at Woolwich, and the *Mary Rose* was laid up in a dock at Deptford. Between 1524 and 1525 she had a skeleton crew of 17 men under the command of Fadere Conner, ship keeper. With the fleet having been in

Fig 94 The departure from Calais showing Calais Harbour, and Henry's army and navy.

ordinary for a number of years, Henry ordered a review in October 1526. The review highlighted that the *Mary Rose* required caulking 'from the keel upward, both within and without', while the *Sovereign* was to be 'new made' from the keel upward. By the end of 1526 the *Mary Rose* was considered 'good for war', except for calking of her orlop, summercastle and decks. The *Mary Rose* had a skeleton crew of eight men in November 1526.

During 1526 certain building works were carried out in Portsmouth. In 1526 nine acres of land were bought by Henry to dig a new dock, build storehouses and make 'vices' for winding the ships into the dock or onto hard ground either side of the docks. The whole area was to be surrounded by a hedge and ditch, with gates for access. The dock was dug early in 1527 with labourers working with the tides. Each labourer was paid 2d per tide.

The *Mary Rose* had to be repaired again in 1527. In June and July of that year she was being repaired, having her overlop and decks fore and aft (in the castles) caulked, along with her outer hull planking from the keel upwards. Not to be left alone, her boat was repaired and trimmed. All this required 37ft of 5in thick planking for her hull, 120ft of 2in planking for the overlop deck and 46ft of squared timber, possibly to replace deck beams and frames. All of this was fastened with numerous nails of various sizes including 'overlop nails' and 'scupper nails'. The caulking consisted of 6¾ hundredweight of oakum, eight barrels of tar and some 'thrums' (sheepskin used in caulking) all supplied by Thomas Jermyn 'Clerk of our sovereign lord'. After this repair, little is known about the *Mary Rose*. There is only one known reference to the *Mary Rose* between late 1528 and 1539. This is in a document written in 1536 by Cromwell, which he states that, among the 'Things done by the King's highness sythyn [since] I came to his service' the *Mary Rose* and six other warships were 'new made'. It is possible that the *Mary Rose* had been rebuilt or at least had extensive repairs, but it is also plausible that this literally refers to things that Cromwell considered himself to have been involved in since he started serving the King. Therefore he could be referring to the repairs of 1527. There is no archaeological evidence that the *Mary Rose* was totally rebuilt as suggested by some. Indeed the dendrochronological evidence suggests to the contrary. While extensive repairs were carried out throughout her career, possibly including repairing the keel and replacing significant amounts of framing, at no time was the hull of the ship (her overall shape being length, depth or breath) changed in any way. It is also highly unlikely that the castles were reduced in any way.

Prelude to war, 1539–1544

While the *Mary Rose* lay idle on the Thames, Henry was busy with his primary concern, the need for a male heir to ensure the secession. With his queen proving to be unable to provide a male heir, Henry naturally started to look for reasons and more significantly another queen. The ensuing politics concerned with Henry's need for another queen resulted in his divorce from his queen, the break with Rome and the Roman Catholic faith, and finally the dissolution of the monasteries. Henry's Dissolution of the Monasteries was not well received and led to unrest in 1536 and 1537. Neither was Rome impressed with his break from their teachings and called on all Christians to attack and destroy the King in 1538. In 1539 Francis I of France and Emperor Charles V of Spain agreed a pact to oppose Henry.

Henry was not naive to the consequence of his actions. As such Henry had taken the precaution of having his fleet, including the *Mary Rose,* prepared for possible use. On 26 January 1539 the *Mary Rose* is noted as '…new made…' and along with the rest of the fleet '…standing in their docks there, masts ready but not set up…' beside the River Thames. As part of his preparations for war Francis I had gathered intelligence about England's readiness for war. This included information about the strength of the English navy, Francis was informed Henry had prepared his ships, which commonly numbered 30 to 40 ships the year before, in anticipation of war. He was also told that the *Henry Grace à Dieu*, *Mary Rose* and *Peter Pomegranate* were by far the largest ships in the fleet.

As part of his continued preparations for war Henry had a book made, dated 13 February 1541, which listed all his ordnance in his castles and on his ships. This book listed the guns on board the *Mary Rose* and notes an increase in the armament of the *Mary Rose* including port pieces, demi-cannons, culverins and demi-culverins. In 1543 we again hear of Henry's preparations for the coming hostilities. A report to the Queen of Hungary on 31 July 1543 stated that Henry was equipping his ships with an incredible quantity of artillery, including six double cannons for the *Mary Rose*. There is a document in the Cecil Papers currently held in the Hatfield House archives (CP 201/127) and transcribed by Charles Knighton. This document is assumed to date from 1545 (though it could be earlier) and is a reply from the King's master shipwright James Baker to Henry's request to add more heavy ordnance firing forward on three of his ships, including the *Mary Rose*. James states that 'First the[re can be] no more [or]dnance laid

Fig 95 A detail from the departure from Calais showing Henry's ships, possibly including the *Mary Rose*.

Fig 96 An attack on Brighton and Hove, which took place before the Battle of the Solent.

at the luff without the taking away of two kn[ees] and the spoiling of the clamps that [c]o[v]ereth the bits, which will be a great weakening to the same part of the ship'. He goes on to state that '…she [the *Mary Rose*] hath right over the luff two whole slings lying forwards over quarter-wise, and at the barbican head likewise forward over two culverins, and the decks over the same shooting likewise forward over two sakers'. All the constructional features described by James are traceable in the archaeological record, the luff being the area just aft of the sterncastle (currently the most forward part of the ship in the Museum). The two knees and clamps covering the bits are still in place. Therefore, although Henry was known to have described James Baker as a simple man, James showed his expertise in ship construction and won his argument. The document shows the King's keen personal interest in his ships and also his want to arm them with more and more heavy ordnance.

Third French War, 1544–1545

The English warships had been brought out of ordinary and placed on standby from 1539 until 1544 when they supported Henry's troops in the capture of Boulogne. It is not known where the *Mary Rose* wintered in 1544–1545, but by the summer of 1545 she is listed with 14 other ships with Sir George Carew as captain. A battle plan drawn up some time around 20 June as part of the ill-fated attack on the French fleet gathered in the Seine lists the *Mary Rose* in the fleet. The attack never materialised due to the usual problem of contrary weather. On 24 June Lisle wrote to the Council telling them that the fleet had been battered by storms and 'strainable

Fig 98 A contemporary chart of Portsmouth Harbour and approaches.

winds'. Parts of the fleet were to be found off the Isle of Wight but the *Mary Rose* and the *Henry Grace à Dieu* were in the Downs awaiting the army coming out of the Thames.

By July the army and the fleet were at Portsmouth. The army was camped at Southsea just outside of Portsmouth town, while the larger part of the navy was moored at Spithead, with a reserve in Portsmouth Harbour. By now the weather had turned for the better, becoming a hot summer. It would not be long before the French were to add to the heat of the day. On the 18 July, on the day before the sinking of the *Mary Rose*, the French arrived off the Isle of Wight and attacked the English navy in Portsmouth.

References
Matthew, HCG and Harrison, B, *Oxford Dictionary of National Biography*, Vol 28, Oxford University Press, 2004

Fig 97 A reproduction of a gun station on the orlop deck of *Mary Rose*.

Henry with his fleet and army was prepared and awaiting the arrival of the French. Viscount Lisle, while making preparations for the forthcoming battle, compiled a plan in expectation of the fight. The day before the first major engagement (Friday 17 July), the French advance guard of four galleys appeared off St Helens Bay, followed later by the rest of the fleet. They anchored in St Helens Road on the north-east corner of the Isle of Wight. The King was holding a banquet aboard his flagship the *Great Harry*. This would have been around about midday. He had asked all his captains to attend, along with Admiral Sir John Dudley, Viscount Lisle, Sir George Carew, who that day was appointed vice-admiral, and was serving on the *Mary Rose*, and no doubt a number of other noble friends. They probably discussed Lisle's orders for the forthcoming battle. During the banquet Henry asked someone to climb the rigging and tell him what they could see. Seemingly Peter Carew dutifully applied and no sooner had he climbed the rigging did he see a number of ships off the Isle of Wight. At first he assumed them to be merchant ships, but soon it became evident that they were indeed the French fleet.

Henry quickly ordered an end to the dinner, sending his captains back to their ships while he returned to the safety of his army, encamped on Southsea Common. Even with the tide this would have taken up to an hour or so, making early afternoon the earliest before the captains were back aboard their ships. More probably it would have been late afternoon, by which time a land wind was blowing and the local tide in and around Portsmouth had turned. This allowed 14 English vessels to stand out of Portsmouth and face the assembling French fleet. A long-distance artillery duel ensued. On behalf of the English ships it was probably nothing more than a show of bravado than anything else. By early evening the English ships retired back to Portsmouth on the flood tide.

The following day, Saturday 18 July, the French set out to engage the English fleet offering a screen for the landing of troops on the Isle of Wight. The lead French ships were the galleys and these closed with and then engaged with the English fleet moving forwards on the tide. The rest of the French fleet, anchored off the eastern side of the Isle of Wight, landed part of the army. The main part of the English fleet, the battle, was already moored in the outer harbour, later termed Spithead anchorage. A further 14 ships, possibly the wing held in reserve in the harbour itself, came out to support the rest of the fleet. The English held a very strong defensive position under the protective shelter of the forts on one side and the hidden bars and shoals on another. The fleet protected the entrance to Portsmouth while being able to respond to any attempt by the French to land forces

THE ENCAM

along the northern coast of the Solent, or to follow it out east or west along the Channel. The first day's battle ended with the French retreating back to their fleet and the English still moored in front of Portsmouth Harbour.

Overnight the French Admiral and his captains decided on a ruse to draw the English fleet out of its defensive position. He would use the galleys as bait to draw the English out into the open seas, where the larger French fleet could get to grips with them. On the second day, Sunday 19 July, the French galleys came forward on the tide to attack the English again. It was a hot summer's day and there was little wind for the English fleet to use. It would appear that they lay motionless at the mercy of the French until later in the afternoon when a sea breeze developed and the tide turned. This happened about 5pm in the late afternoon (M[c]Elvogue 2007). Then the English fleet could venture forward and attack the French. This would mean raising the anchors prior to setting the sails. To raise the anchors would require the seaman to man the capstans and would have taken at least an hour. Furthermore the sails would have to have been made ready, utilising the rest of the seamen. The far quicker method was to set the sails and let go the anchors, letting them lie where they were and come back for them

...NT OF THE ENGLISH FORCES NEAR PORTSMOUTH,

The Battle of the Solent

The Cowdray engraving that depicts the loss of the *Mary Rose* is one of a set of 5 images recording Henry VIII's war with France 1544–1545. Most likely made between 1545 and 1548 for Sir Anthony Browne, master of the King's horse, it hung on the walls of the dining hall at Cowdry House, Midhurst, Sussex. Sir Anthony Browne, a wealthy and well-connected man – is shown prominently in the centre of the image just behind King Henry VIII. He is riding a fine white horse alongside Sir Charles Brandon, first Duke of Suffolk, commander of the English land forces at Portsmouth.

The Cowdry Engraving of Portsmouth is a bird's-eye view looking over Southsea and the Solent with the Isle of Wight beyond. The bottom of the image shows the English encampment, with Henry VIII and Sir Anthony Browne in the middle. Above them is Southsea Castle, the guns of which are firing to sea at the French galleys which are harrying the English fleet. At the front of the fleet and firing back at the French galleys is the *Henry Grace à Dieu*, and just below it the mast of the already sunk *Mary Rose*. The rest of the English fleet lies to the right at Spithead, with the French fleet to the left lying at St Helen's Roads. Ashore on the Isle of Wight we can see French and English forces. Much maligned, the Cowdry engraving is now seen as an accurate illustration of the main protagonists and the position for the sinking of the *Mary Rose* at Spithead.

at a later date. In the meantime the soldiers and gunners would prepare themselves and their stations for action.

Once underway, the ship could close the range and use her cannon on the galleys. At least some of the ordnance was fired (if not an actual full broadside) on the *Mary Rose*, most probably her long-range culverins, after which she turned to fire those on her other side. This whole evolution would take at least 15 minutes to accomplish, from giving the order to prepare to go about, to actually going about and having everything made fast again and the ship lying on the new course (McElvogue 2007). During this time it would appear that the *Mary Rose* suffered some misfortune, which made her heal heavily to starboard and ultimately resulted in her sinking.

Fig 99 Detail from the Cowdry engraving of the sinking of the *Mary Rose*.

Cast away

Soon after the loss, the Imperial ambassador to Charles V, Van der Delft, interviewed a survivor of the sinking. In a letter to Charles V, dated 23/4 July (Spanish Calendar, VIII), Van der Delft tells us what that survivor told him:

'Towards evening, through misfortune and carelessness, the ship of Vice-Admiral George Carew foundered, and all hands on board, to the number of about 500, were drowned, with the exception of about five and twenty or thirty servants, sailors and the like, who escaped. I made enquires of one of the survivors, a Fleming, how the ship perished, and he told me that the disaster was caused by their not having closed the lowest row of gunports on one side of the ship. Having fired the guns on that side, the ship was turning, in order to fire from the other, when the wind caught her sails so strongly as to heel her over, and plunge her open gunports beneath the water, which flooded and sank her. They say, however, that they can recover the ship and guns.'

At the same time Lord Russell wrote to Sir William Paget (23 July) stating that the *Mary Rose* had been lost '…through such rashness and great negligence'. The French in the guise of Martin du Bellay, understandably claimed they sank the *Mary Rose* by gunfire, with the loss of all but 35 men. Three years later Hall, in his Chronicle c1548, tells us that the *Mary Rose* was sunk 'by to much foly … for she was laden with much ordinaunce, and

the portes left open, which were low…so that when the ship should turne, the water entered, and sodainly she sanke.' More importantly he adds that the guns were un-breached. This appears to be repeated by Hollingshed's in his account c1577 stating that: 'One of the King's shippes, called the Marye Rose, was drowned in the myddest of the haven, by reason that she was overladen with ordinaunce, and had the portes lefte open, whiche were very lowe, and the great artillerie unbreeched, so that when the ship shoolde tourne, the water entred, and soddainely she sunke. In hir [her] was Sir George Carewe, knight, and foure hundreth souldioures under his guidyng. There escaped not paste fortie persons of all the number.'

Most of the myth that surrounds the sinking of the *Mary Rose* comes from the account by Richard Hooker (c1575) in his biography of Sir Peter Carew written almost 30 years after the sinking. It is Hooker who claims the ship carried 700 men, which is clearly an overestimation when compared to all other contemporary accounts. Apart from this we do get more detail concerning the operations. Hooker tells us that:

'Sir George Carewe being entered into his shippe, commaunded everye man to take his place, and the sayles to be hoysed, but the same was noe sonner donne, but that the Marye Roose beganne to heele, that is, to leane one the one syde. Sir Gawen Carewe beinge then in his own shipp, and seeinge the same, called for the master of his shippe, and tolde hyme there of, and asked hyme what it mente, who awenssweared, that yf shee did heele, she was lycke to be caste awaye. Then the sayd Sir Gawen, passinge by Marye Roose, called oute to Sir George Carewe, askeinge hyme howe he did, who answered, that he had a sorte of knaves whom he could not rule. And it was not lounge after but that the sayde Mary Roose, thus heelinge more and more, was drowned, with 700 men wiche were in here, whereof very fewe escaped.'

Hooker does not mention firing of guns, neither does Hall, nor the gunport lids being left open, and although he adds further detail this should be considered with some hesitation. In any case, the ship sank with virtually all hands late in the afternoon on 19 July 1545.

Contemporary salvage, c1545–1549

From the start, plans were discussed and put in place to raise the ship, with Charles Brandon, Duke of Suffolk, in charge. In consultation with a Venetian salvager, possibly already working on wrecks in the Solent, a list of equipment needed was made. This included: two great hulks, four great hoys, lengths of the greatest cable available, with capstans and pulleys, 60 ballast baskets, and 40lb of tallow as well as 30 of the best Venetian seamen and one Venetian carpenter as salvors. The aim was to right the ship by using her masts to lever her upright, then pass a series of cables attached to the great hulks under the hull. At low water the slack would be taken in and on a rising tide the *Mary Rose* would be lifted and taken further inshore.

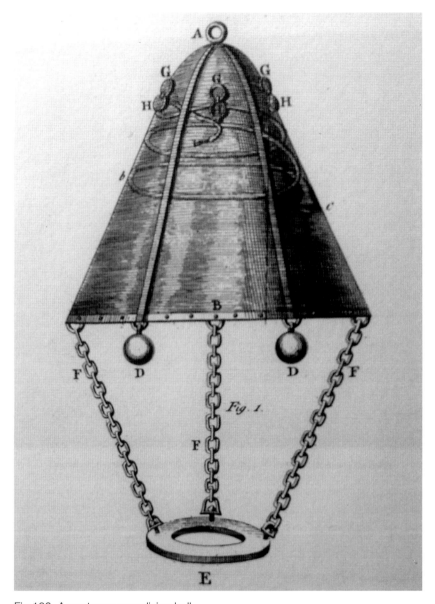

Fig 100 A contemporary diving bell.

still continued to work the site until 1549, salvaging as many guns as was possible.

By the end of 1549 it would appear that all salvage work had ceased and thereafter the *Mary Rose* was abandoned. By this time Henry had already died (Friday 28 January, 1547). The expenses for attempting to raise the *Mary Rose*, as noted in the accounts for expenditure in Henry's reign, were;

'Charges of the *Mary Rose* which was drowned at Portsmouth, the weighing whereof with the recovery of some parts of her tackling, anchors and ordnance, cost in The said late King's time £559 8s 7d.'

More interestingly, a cost was put on the loss of the ordnance of the *Mary Rose*:

'Ordinance with munitions and habiliaments of war spent, lost and employed in the King's Majesty's ships serving upon the seas within all the time of the said wars. Viz in: The said King's time with £1,723 2s of the price of certain ordnance lost in the *Mary Rose* at Portsmouth.' (Knighton and Loades 2002).

References
Calendar of State Papers, Spain, VIII, No 101
McElvogue, DM, *The Fateful Day*, unpublished lecture notes and
    PowerPoint, Mary Rose Trust, 2007

Thus in stages the ship would slowly be transported underwater closer to Portsmouth dock, where eventually she would be pumped out and floated.

Suffolk started the salvage attempts on 3 August, and by next day they had managed to cut away some of the sails and yards, which he laid out to dry. They tried to right the *Mary Rose* on 6 August but failed, so tried again on 8 August. By the next day, having broken the foremast, they concluded they could not recover the ship. By now she might already have begun to silt up, the weight of which was acting against the salvors. After August all hopes of raising the ship seem to have been abandoned. A certain Italian, however,

A General arrangements c1511–1545

A1   Body plan (1/96 scale)

A2   Buttock lines (1/192 scale)

A3   Half breadth plan showing waterlines (1/192 scale)

1   Forecastle
2   Waist
3   Stern castle

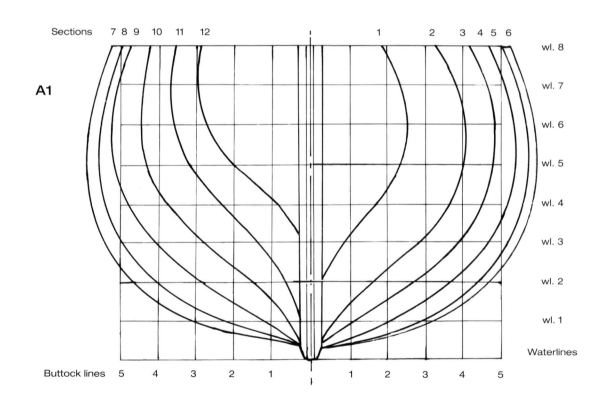

A2

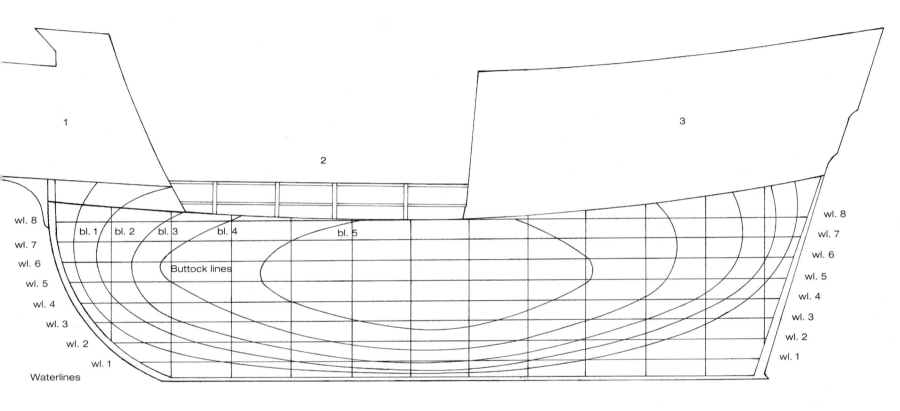

wl. 8
wl. 7
wl. 6
wl. 5
wl. 4
wl. 3
wl. 2
wl. 1

bl. 1   bl. 2   bl. 3   bl. 4   bl. 5

Buttock lines

wl. 8
wl. 7
wl. 6
wl. 5
wl. 4
wl. 3
wl. 2
wl. 1

Waterlines

A3

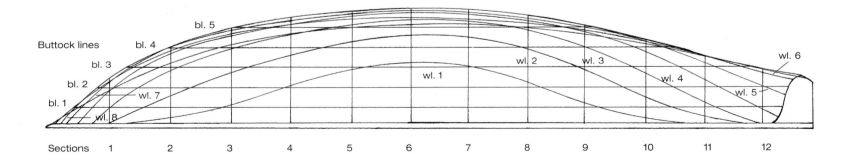

Buttock lines

bl. 5
bl. 4
bl. 3
bl. 2
bl. 1

wl. 7
wl. 8

wl. 1

wl. 2   wl. 3

wl. 4

wl. 6

wl. 5

Sections   1   2   3   4   5   6   7   8   9   10   11   12

63

B Hull construction c1511–1545

The building sequence

B1   Phase 1 – keel, quarter and master frame floors and floors between the quarter frames. Keelson and lower part of apron (1/192 scale)

B2   Phase 2 – lower stem, stern post assemblage and inner wale (1/192 scale)

B3   Phase 3 – stempost assemblage, transom assemblage, first futtocks and inner wale (1/192 scale)

B4   Phase 4 – second futtocks and external wale (1/192 scale)

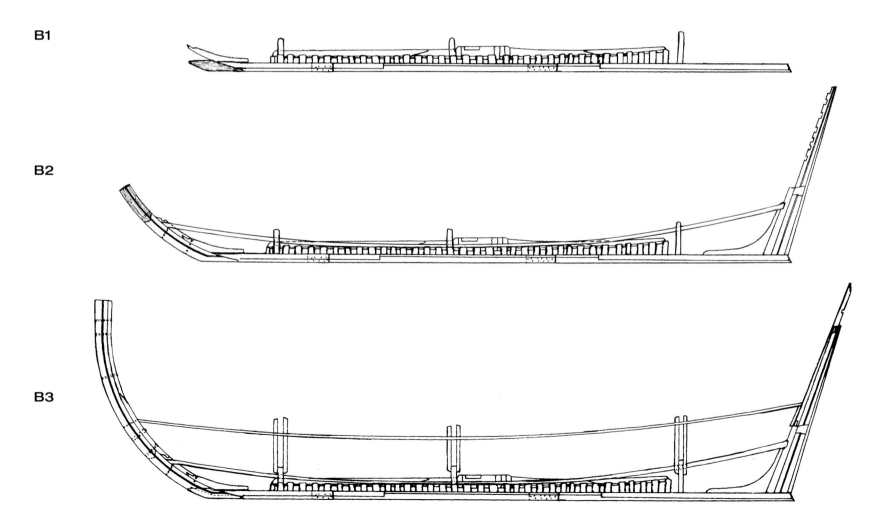

B1

B2

B3

64

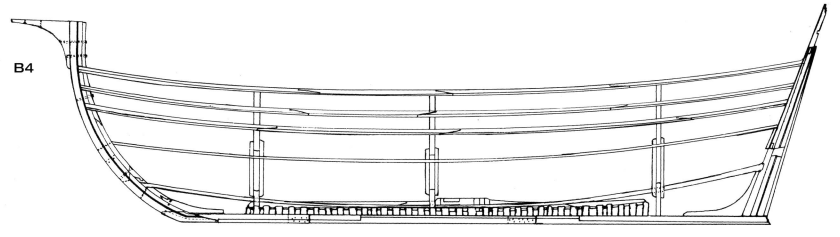

B4

B5   Keel sections (1) fore (2) mid (3) aft (1/96 scale)

B6   Keelson sections (1) fore (2) mid (3) aft (1/96 scale)

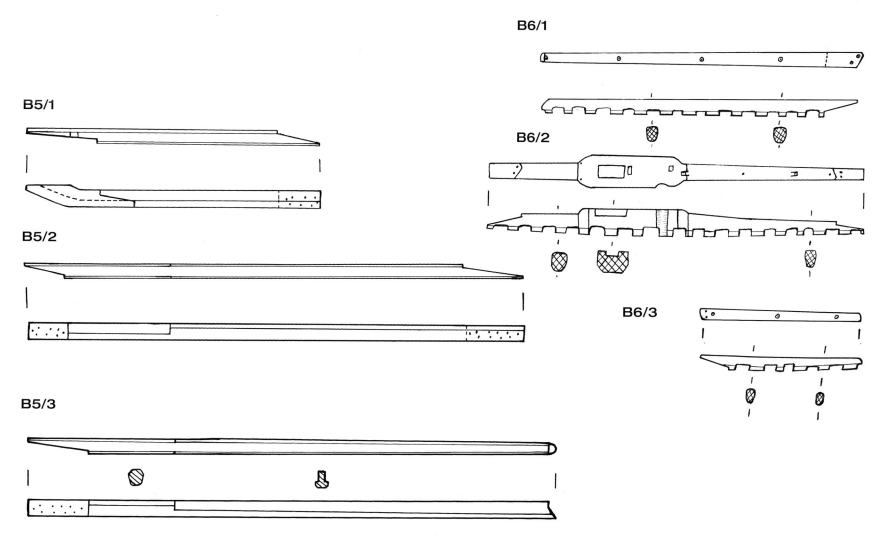

B6/1

B5/1

B6/2

B5/2

B6/3

B5/3

B Hull construction c1511–1545

B7 Mast step detail
(1/96 scale)

1 Mast step
2 Side supports
3 Stanchion mortice
4 Bolt holes
5 Scarf
6 Cut out for pump

B8 Stempost assemblage
(1/48 scale)

B9 Stempost components
(no scale)

1 Knee
2 Through bolts
3 Upper stempiece
4 Sully scarf
5 Lower stempiece
6 Stem to keel scarf

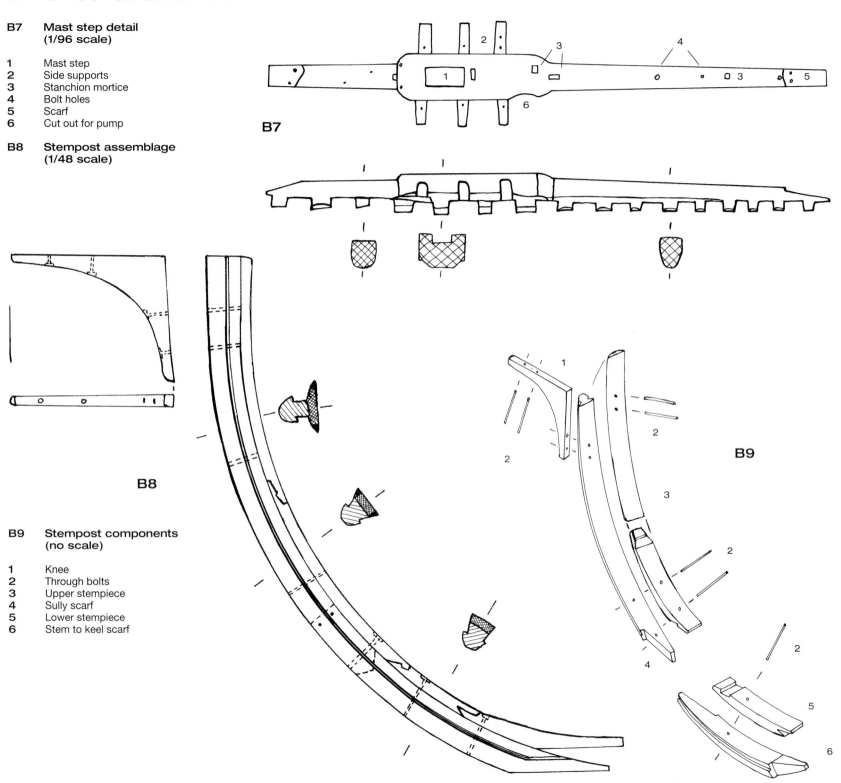

B7

B8

B9

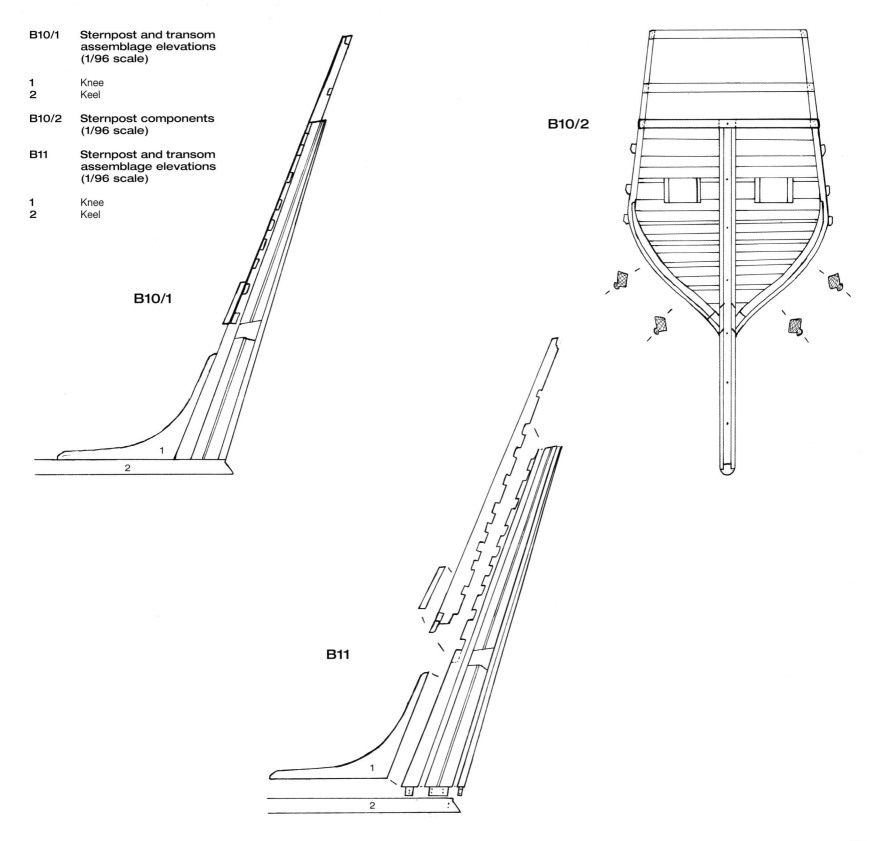

B10/1 Sternpost and transom
assemblage elevations
(1/96 scale)

1 Knee
2 Keel

B10/2 Sternpost components
(1/96 scale)

B11 Sternpost and transom
assemblage elevations
(1/96 scale)

1 Knee
2 Keel

B10/1

B10/2

B11

B Hull construction c1511–1545

B12   Fore quarter frame (1/96 scale)

B13   Aft quarter frame (1/96 scale)

B14   Master frame (1/72 scale)

1   Keel
2   Floor
3   Rider
4   1st futtock
5   2nd futtock
6   False overlop
7   Overlop deck beam
8   Waist beam
9   Waist
10   Limber hole
11   Garboard strake
12   Caulking seam
13   Outer hull planking
14   Ceiling planking
15   'Thick stuff' or stringer
16   Keelson
17   Deck clamp
18   Shelf
19   Stringer
20   Standing knee
21   Carlings
22   Stanchion
23   Ledge
24   Lodging knee
25   Hatch
26   Hull planking
27   Wale
28   Gunwale

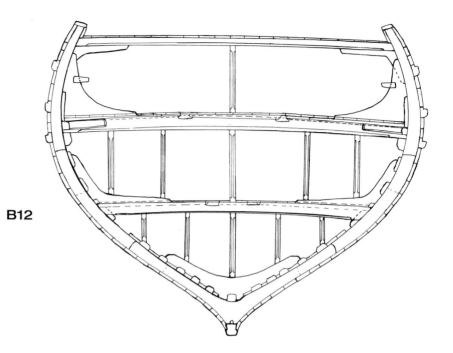

B12

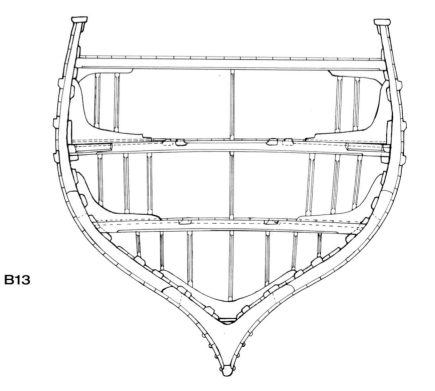

B13

B14

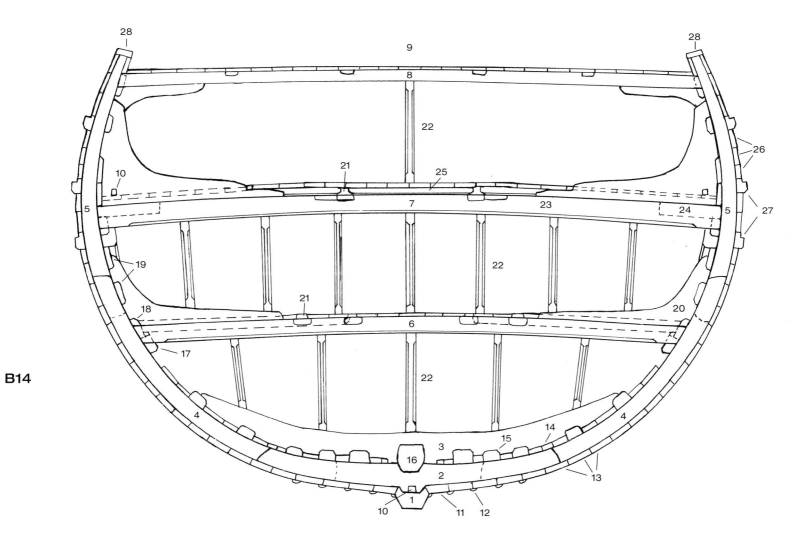

B Hull construction c1511–1545

B15   External elevation 1511 (1/192 scale)

B16   Internal elevation 1511 (1/192 scale)

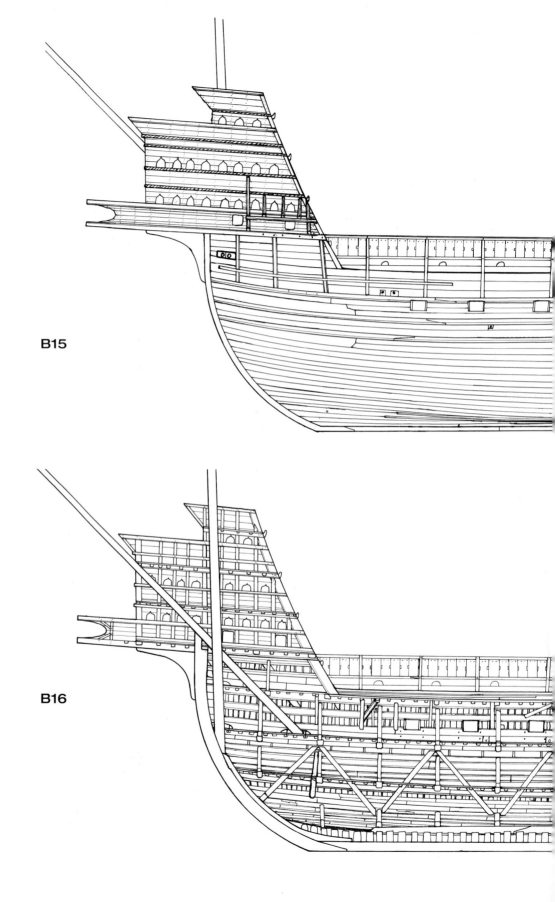

B15

B16

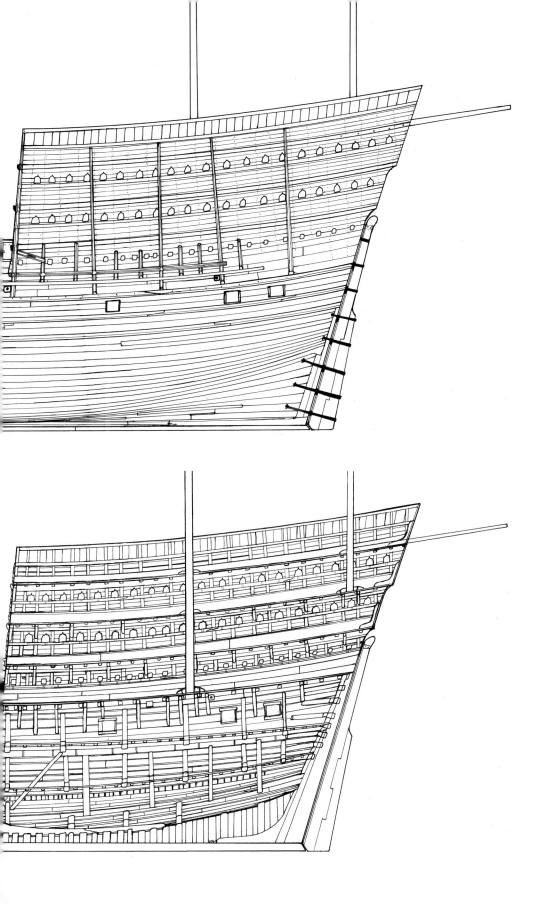

B Hull construction c1511–1545

B17   Forecastle 1511 (1/96 scale)

1   Highest deck
2   Upper forecastle
3   Forecastle
4   Bowsprit
5   Hawse holes

B18   Barbican 1511 (1/96 scale)

1   Highest deck
2   Upper forecastle
3   Forecastle
4   Companionway on cubbridge head
5   Guttering
6   Nether deck
7   Orlop deck
8   Lower orlop
9   Hold

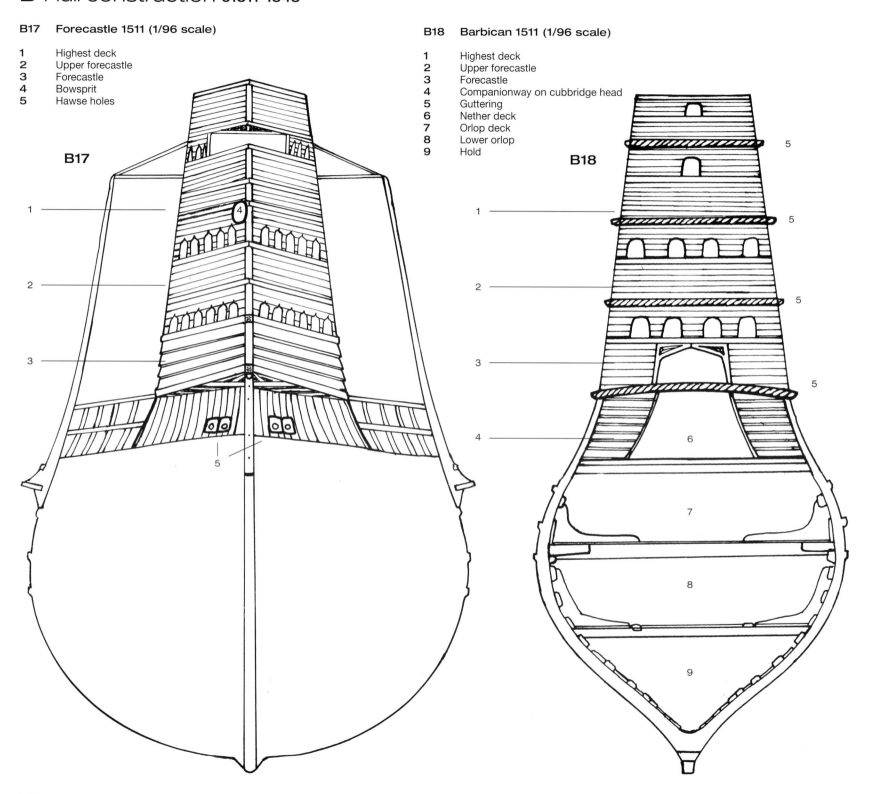

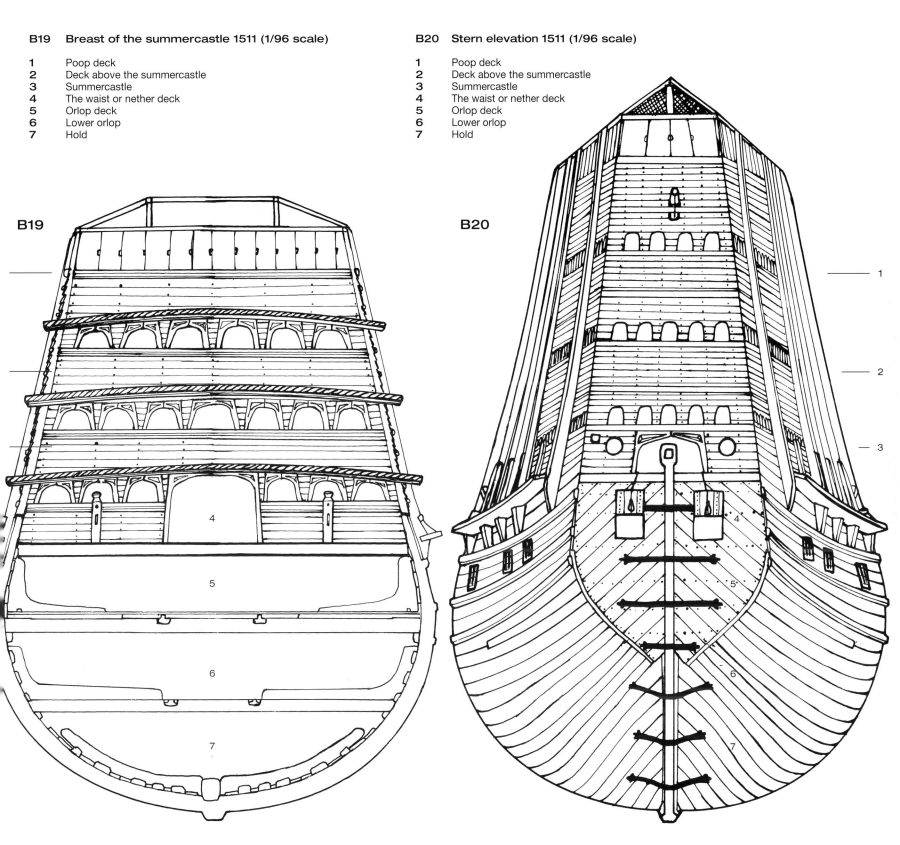

B19   **Breast of the summercastle 1511 (1/96 scale)**

1   Poop deck
2   Deck above the summercastle
3   Summercastle
4   The waist or nether deck
5   Orlop deck
6   Lower orlop
7   Hold

B20   **Stern elevation 1511 (1/96 scale)**

1   Poop deck
2   Deck above the summercastle
3   Summercastle
4   The waist or nether deck
5   Orlop deck
6   Lower orlop
7   Hold

B Hull construction c1511-1545

B21 Forecastle 1545 (1/96 scale)

1 Highest deck
2 Upper forecastle
3 Forecastle
4 Bowsprit
5 Hawse holes
6 Added gun positions

B22 Barbican 1545 (1/96 scale)

1 Highest deck
2 Upper forecastle
3 Forecastle
4 Companionway on cubbridge head
5 Guttering
6 Nether deck
7 Orlop deck
8 Lower orlop
9 Hold
10 Added gun positions

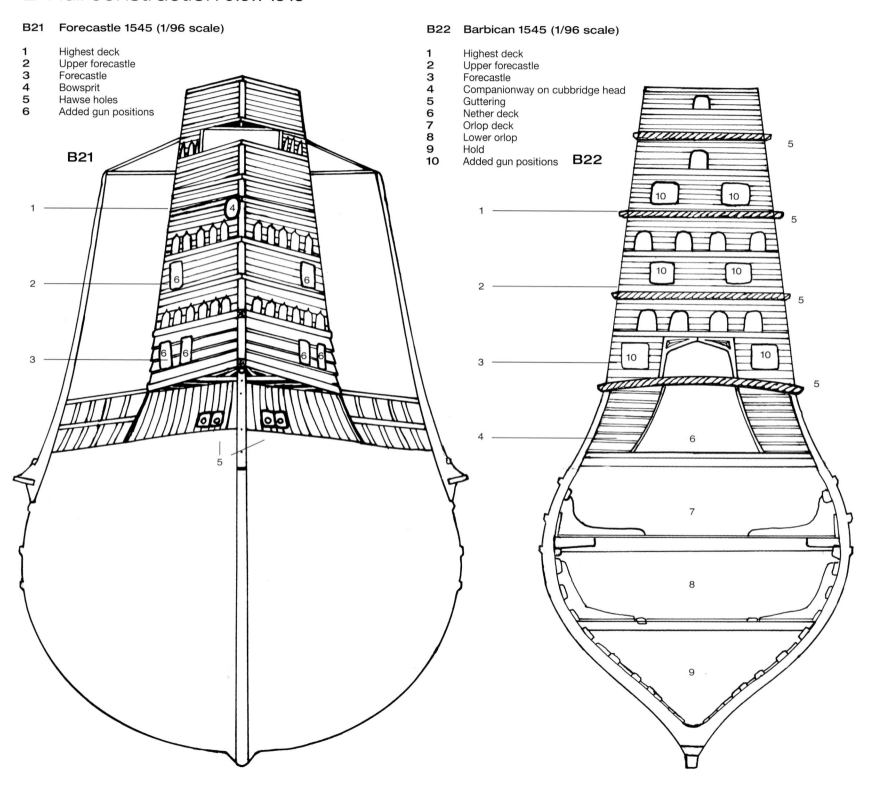

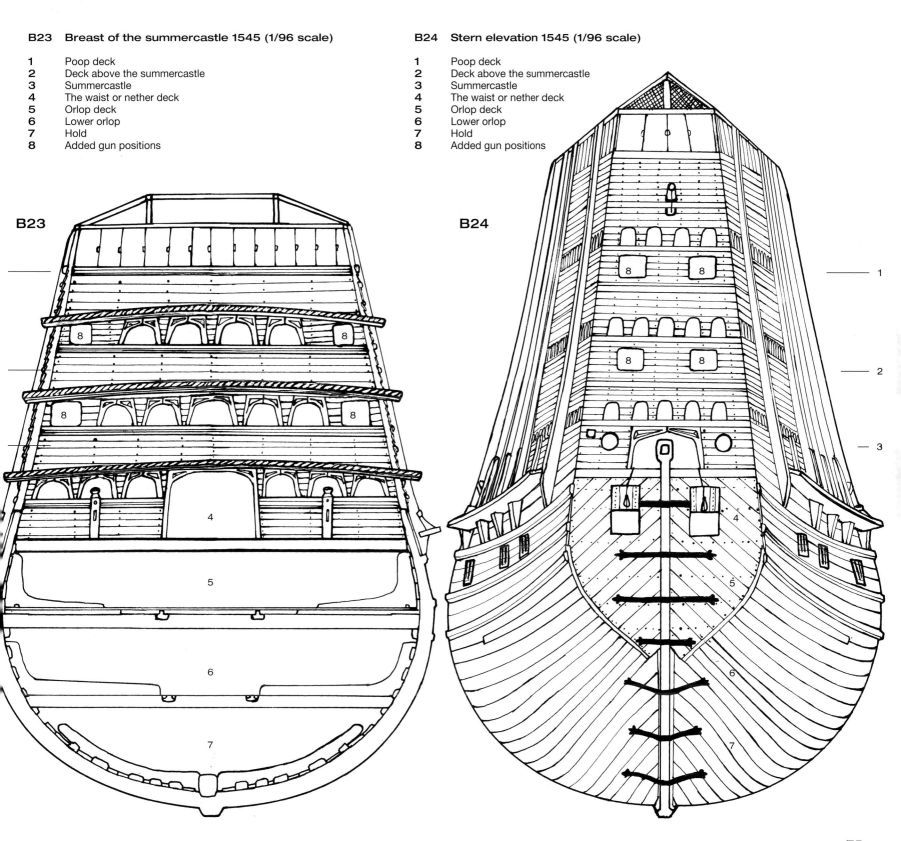

B23 Breast of the summercastle 1545 (1/96 scale)

1 Poop deck
2 Deck above the summercastle
3 Summercastle
4 The waist or nether deck
5 Orlop deck
6 Lower orlop
7 Hold
8 Added gun positions

B24 Stern elevation 1545 (1/96 scale)

1 Poop deck
2 Deck above the summercastle
3 Summercastle
4 The waist or nether deck
5 Orlop deck
6 Lower orlop
7 Hold
8 Added gun positions

B23

B24

B Hull construction c1511–1545

B25   Hold (1/192 scale)

1	Stempost
2	Apron
3	Keel
4	Riders
5	Ceiling planking
6	Maststep
7	Main mast
8	Stringers
9	Keelson
10	Pump well
11	Floor
12	Futtocks

B25

B26   False orlop deck (1/192 scale)

1	Stempost
2	Apron
3	Braces
4	Deck planking
5	Smoke hood
6	Main mast
7	Carlings
8	Ledges
9	Pump
10	Standing knees
11	Deck beams
12	Rudder
13	Transom
14	Sternpost
15	Hatchway
16	Hatch covers
17	Mizzen mast

B26

B27 Main orlop deck (1/192 scale)

1   Stempost
2   Foremast
3   Bowsprit partner
4   Base for companionway
5   Gunports
6   Mast partner
7   Carlings
8   Hull planking
9   Pump
10 Standing knees
11 Rudder
12 Transom
13 Transom knee
14 Hatchways
15 Capstan partner
16 Mizzen mast
17 Lodging knees
18 Ledges
19 Breast hook

B27

B28 Forecastle & summercastle nether decks & waist (1/192 scale)

1   Stempost
2   Foremast partner
3   Bowsprit partner
4   Fore chainwale
5   Gunwale
6   Mast partner
7   Scuttles
8   Deck planking
9   Pump

B28

10 Mizzen mast partner
11 Chainwale
12 Transom
13 Aft pump dale
14 Hatchway
15 Midships pump dale
16 Mizzen mast
17 Lodging knees
18 Carlings
19 Ledges
20 Deck beams
21 Forecastle netherdeck
22 Waist
23 Summercastle netherdeck

B Hull construction c1511–1545

B29 Forecastle (1/192 scale)

1 Bowsprit
2 Foremast
3 Deck planking
4 Beams

B30 Upper forecastle deck (1/192 scale)

1 Bowsprit
2 Foremast
3 Deck planking
4 Beams
5 Knee

B31 Highest deck (1/192 scale)

1 Foremast
2 Knee

B32 Deck above the highest deck (1/192 scale)

1 Foremast

B33 Summercastle (1/192 scale)

1 Deck planking
2 Mizzen mast
3 Mast partner
4 Standing knees
5 Lodging knee
6 Ledges

B34 Upper summercastle deck (1/192 scale)

1 Deck planking
2 Mizzen mast
3 Mast partner
4 Standing knees
5 Lodging knee
6 Ledges
7 Bonaventure mast
8 Bonaventure mast partner

B35 Poop deck (1/192 scale)

1 Deck planking
2 Mizzen mast
3 Mast partner
4 Standing knees
5 Lodging knee
6 Ledges
7 Bonaventure mast
8 Bonaventure mast partner

B29

B30

B31

B32

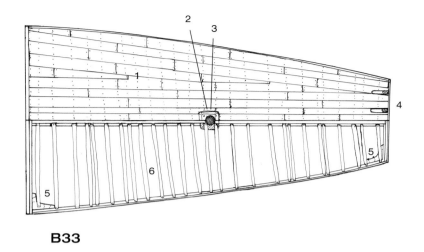

B33

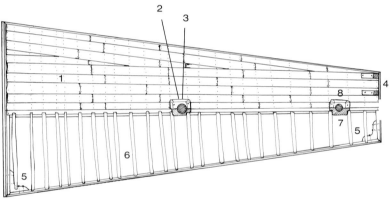

B34

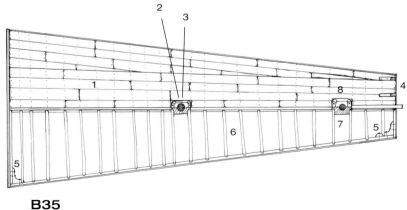

B35

B36 Top rail (no scale)

1   Mortices for anti-boarding netting ledge

B37 Waist and pavises (no scale)

1   Bow
2   Stern
3   Main mast
4   Top rail
5   Rope holes
6   Pavises
7   Handgrip
8   Waist rail or gunwale
9   Standards
10   Gunport
11   Pump dale

B38 Waist rail (1/96 scale)

1   Detail of scarf
2   Tenons for pavises

B39 Waist standards (1/72 scale)

1   Cut out for rail
2   Rebates for rails
3   Bolts
4   Knees

B40 Detail of waist rail and pavises
construction (no scale)

1   Top rail
2   Rail
3   Gunwale

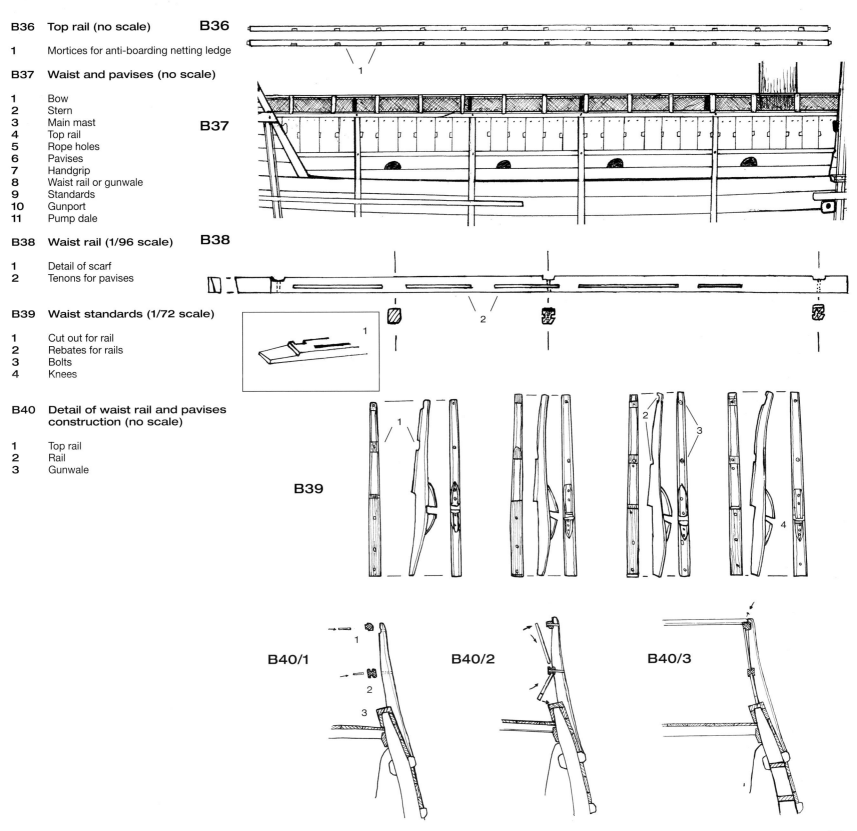

B Hull construction c1511–1545

B41 Top rail joint (no scale)

1 Cut out mortice for nail hole for anti-boarding netting

B42 Pavises (1/72 scale)

1 Holes for rope
2 Handgrips
3 Tenon

B43 Anti-boarding netting support in position (no scale)

1 Anti-boarding netting support
2 Waist deck beam

B44 Anti-boarding netting supports (1/72 scale)

1 Nail
2 Foot support
3 Tenon

B45 Anti-boarding netting joists (1/72 scale)

B46 Anti-boarding netting detail (no scale)

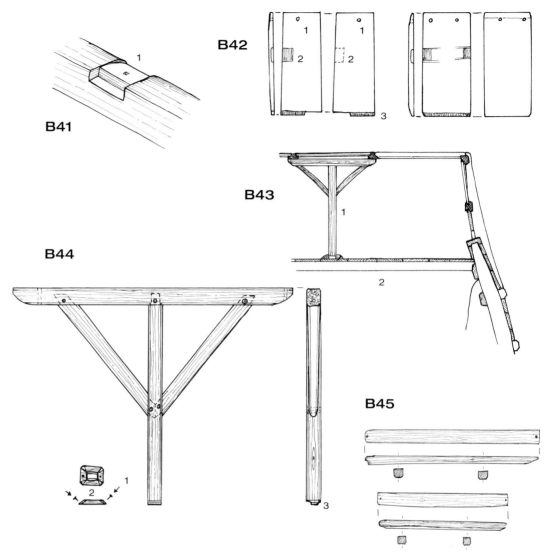

B41

B42

B43

B44

B45

B46/1

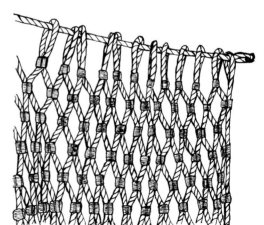

B46/2

80

B47 View of waist area showing gunport
opening arrangement (no scale)

1 Gunport opening rope
2 Gunport
3 Pavises
4 Wale

B48 Gunport (1) external, (2) internal (3) side
elevation (1/72 scale)

1 Gunport ring
2 Gunport ring to shore up port

B49 Gunport construction (no scale)

1 Nails
2 Outer planks
3 Inner planks
4 Rove
5 Gunport hinge
6 Rebate for hinge

B50 Gunport hinge bolted to the upper wale
(no scale)

1 Rove through ring bolt

B48/1 **B48/2** **B48/3**

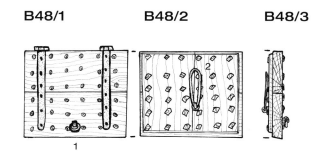

B47

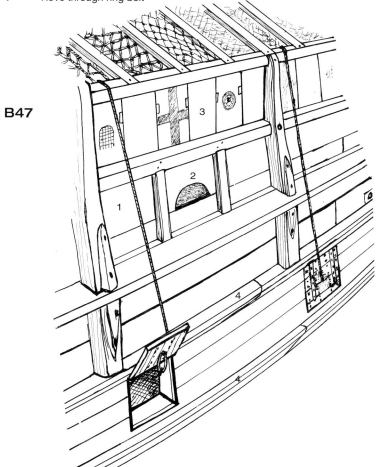

B49/1 **B49/2**

B49/3

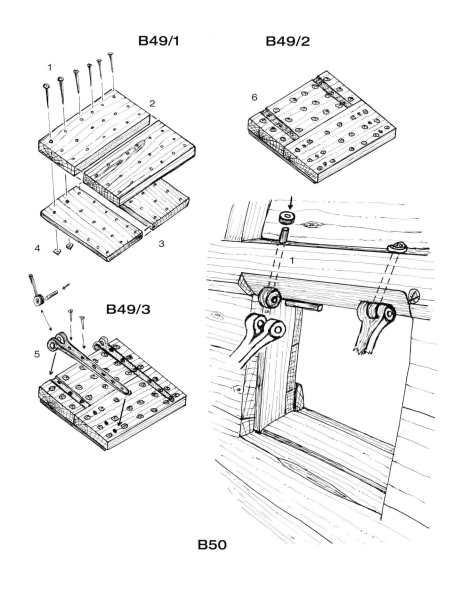

B50

B Hull construction c1511–1545

B51   Knight in the breast of the summercastle
         (1/72 scale)

B52   Knee for the knight in the breast of the
         summercastle (1/72 scale)

B53   knighthead rail in the breast of the
         summercastle (1/72 scale)

B54   Construction of the summercastle
         (section) (no scale)

1   Knight
2   Nail
3   Pavise
4   Middle rail
5   Gunwale
6   Weather boarding
7   Waterway
8   Deck clamp

B55   Constructional elevation for the knight in
         the breast of the summercastle
         (1/24 scale)

1   Top rail
2   Rail
3   Through bolt
4   Knee
5   Bolt for sheave
6   Deck planking
7   Pump dale
8   Deck beam

B56   Summercastle pavises (1/48 scale)

B57   Summercastle fitting of the pavises
         (no scale)

B58   Summercastle gunwale (no scale)

1   Cut out for framing
2   Hole for minche of gun
3   Tenon for pavise
4   Treenails

B51

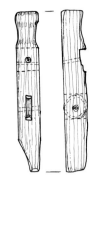

B52

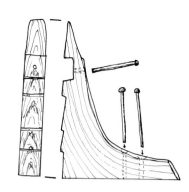

B53

B54

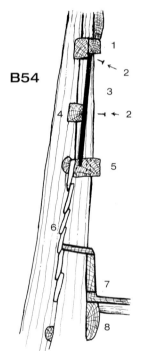

B55

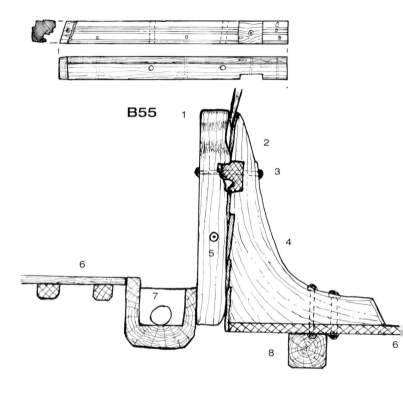

B56

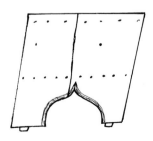

B57

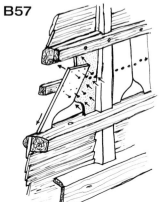

B58

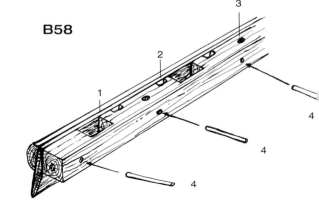

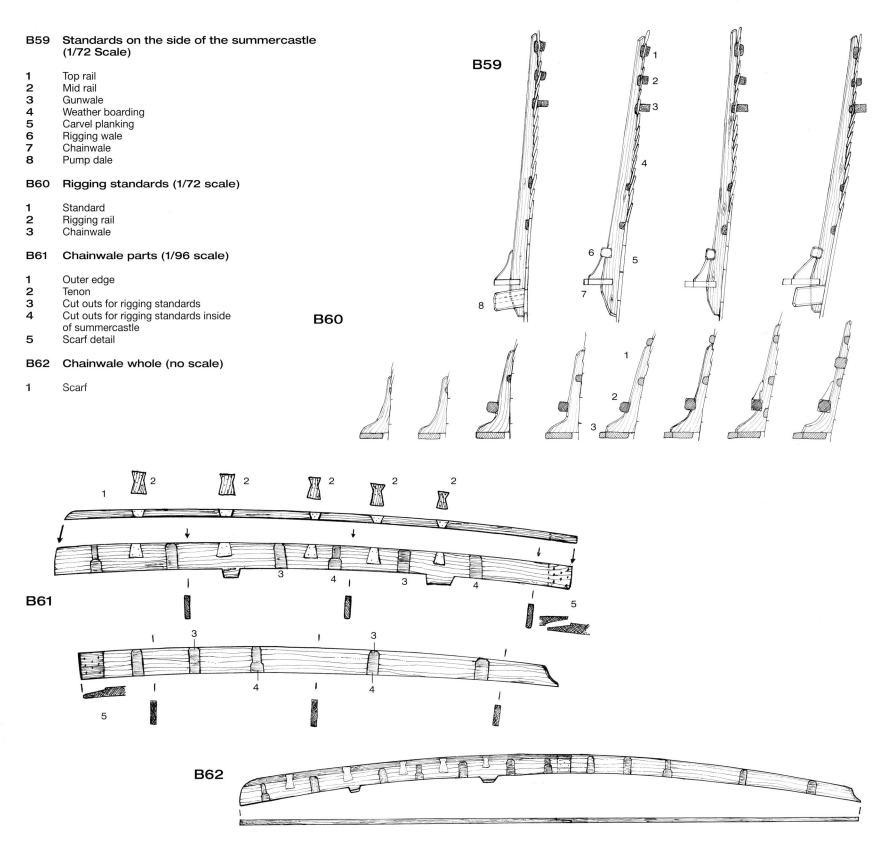

B59 Standards on the side of the summercastle (1/72 Scale)

1 Top rail
2 Mid rail
3 Gunwale
4 Weather boarding
5 Carvel planking
6 Rigging wale
7 Chainwale
8 Pump dale

B60 Rigging standards (1/72 scale)

1 Standard
2 Rigging rail
3 Chainwale

B61 Chainwale parts (1/96 scale)

1 Outer edge
2 Tenon
3 Cut outs for rigging standards
4 Cut outs for rigging standards inside of summercastle
5 Scarf detail

B62 Chainwale whole (no scale)

1 Scarf

B Hull construction c1511–1545

B63   Ladder (1/48 scale)

B64   Companionways (1/48 scale)

B65   Ladder position (1) as reconstructed
       by Mary Rose Trust and (2) as more
       probably positioned (no scale)

B66   Maindeck stanchion and footing for
       stanchion (1/48 scale)

1   Footing for stanchion

B67   Companionway on the overlop deck
       on the forecastle (1) in position (2) side
       elevation (3) construction detail
       (1/48 scale)

B68   Scuttle in the waist over the main overlop
       deck ordnance

1   Ledges
2   Coaming
3   Deck planking

B69   Scuttle cover (no scale)

B70   Scuttle cover construction
       (no scale)

1   Nails
2   Planks
3   Frame

B71   Hatch cover – for false and main orlop
       decks (1/48 scale)

1   Nails
2   Planks
3   Ledge

B72   Hatch in position (no scale)

B63

B64

B65/1

B64

B65/2

B66

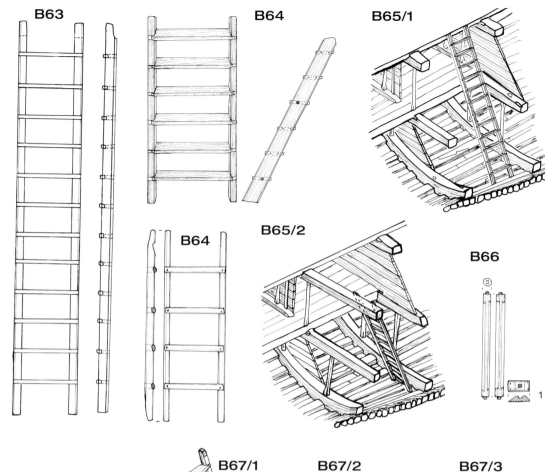

B67/1   **B67/2**   **B67/3**

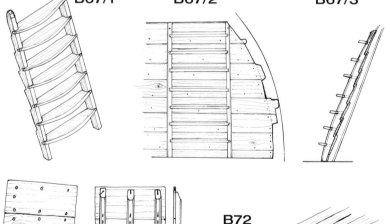

B68   **B69**   **B70**

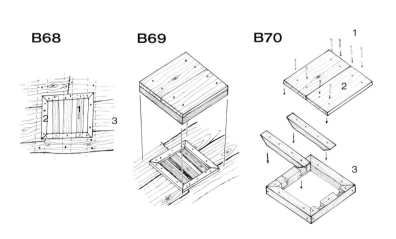

B71

B72

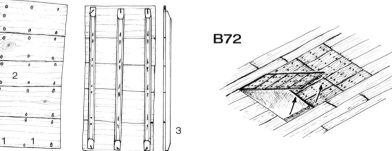

STEERING

B73 Rudder assemblage (1/96 scale)

1 Tiller
2 Pintle
3 Pintle strop
4 Front piece
5 Back piece

B74 Rudder construction (1/96 scale)

B75 Rudder and tiller on stern (1/96 scale)

1 Nether deck
2 Gun deck

B76 Pintle cut out (no scale)

B77 Tiller (1/48 scale)

**B78 Relieving tackle for the rudder
       (no scale)**

1 Single block
2 Double block
3 Hook
4 Eye bolt

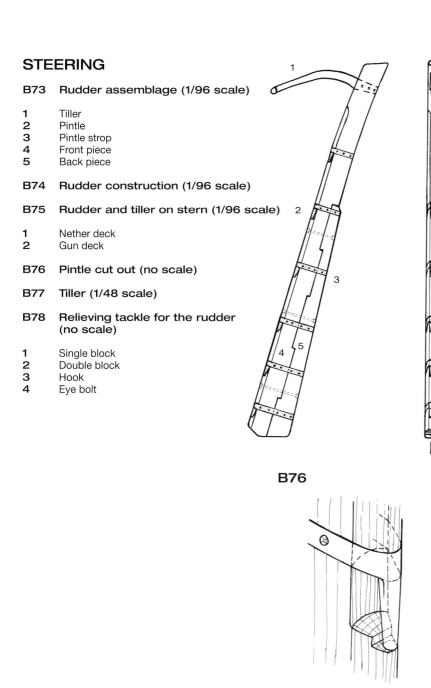

B73

B74

B75

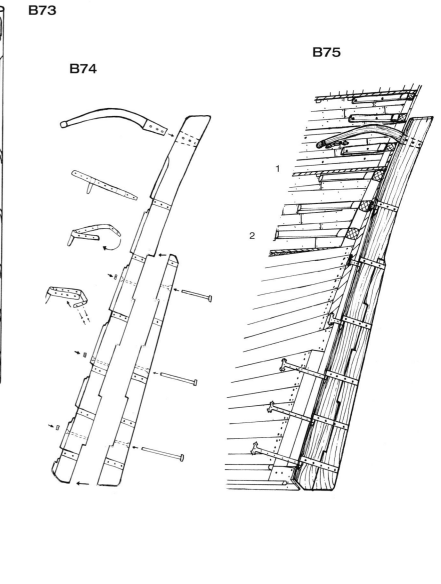

B76

B77

B78

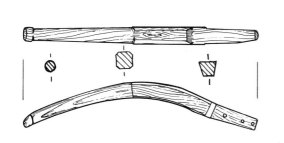

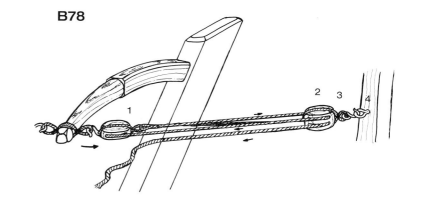

B Hull construction c1511–1545

PUMPING

B79 Pumps in the ship (no scale)

1 Pump 1
2 Pump 2
3 Pump dale

B80 Pump handle assemblage (1/48 scale)

1 Pump brake
2 Top of pump spear
3 Stirrup
4 Pin

B81 Upper pump valve inspection hatch (1/48 scale)

B82 lower part of the pump in the well (no scale)

1 False orlop deck
2 Pump well
3 Bulkhead
4 Ceiling plank
5 Floors
6 Keel

B83 Pump tube (1/96 scale)

B84 Upper pump valve (1/5 scale)

1 Nails for bottom of spear
2 Nails for leather
3 Leather non-return valve
4 Leather valve

B85 Lower pump valve (1/5 scale)

1 Leather flapper
2 Nail
3 Valve box
4 Iron strap
5 Journals for water

B79

B80

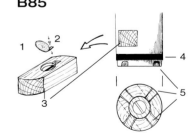

B83

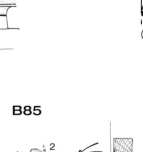

B81

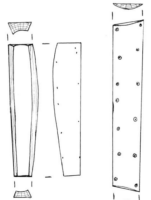

B82

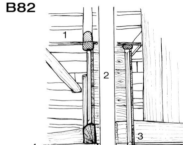

B84

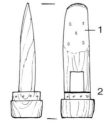

B85

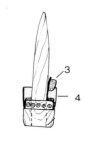

B86 Scupper box in position between the frames (no scale)

B87 Scupper box detail (1/48 scale)

B88 Scupper leather with sewing detail and nail pattern (no scale)

1 Sewing detail
2 Scupper nails

B89 Scupper assemblage (1/5 scale)

1 Leather 1
2 Leather 2
3 Leather seam

B90 Midships and aft dales (no scale)

1 Pump tube
2 Trough
3 Pump dale
4 Side of hull

B91 Dale ending through the side of the hull (no scale)

1 Rigging rail
2 Chainplate
3 Pump dale
4 Standing knee
5 Wale
6 Frame

B92 Detail of the breast of the summercastle gutter (1/24 scale)

1 Weather boarding
2 Guttering
3 Outer hull planking

B93 Leather bucket for bailing out the ship (1/10 scale)

B94 Caulking and seam batten (no scale)

1 Carvel plank
2 Caulking
3 Nail
4 Caulking seam batten
5 Caulking roll or thrum

B86

B87

B88

B89

B90

B91

B92

B93

B94

C Masts and yards

C1 Masts (1/192 scale)

C1

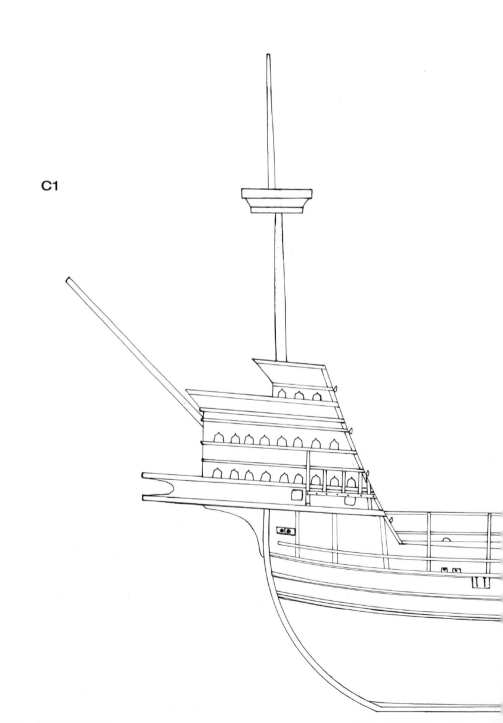

89

C Masts and yards

C2   Standing rigging (1/192 scale)

C2

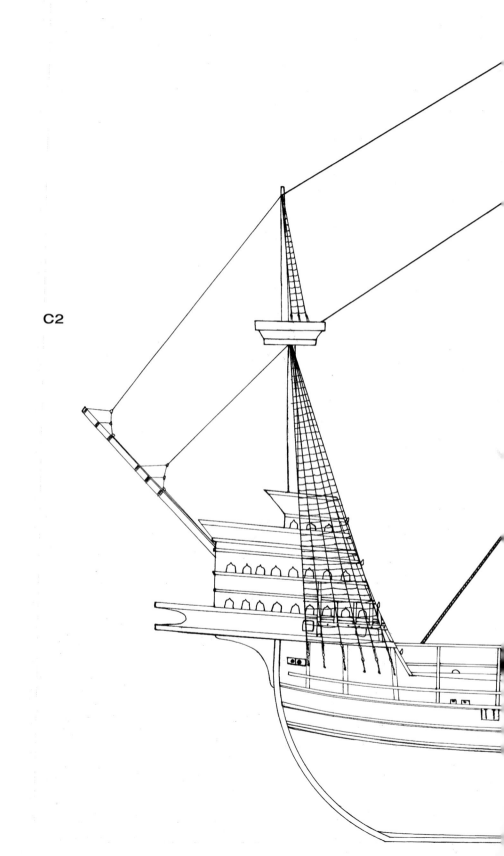

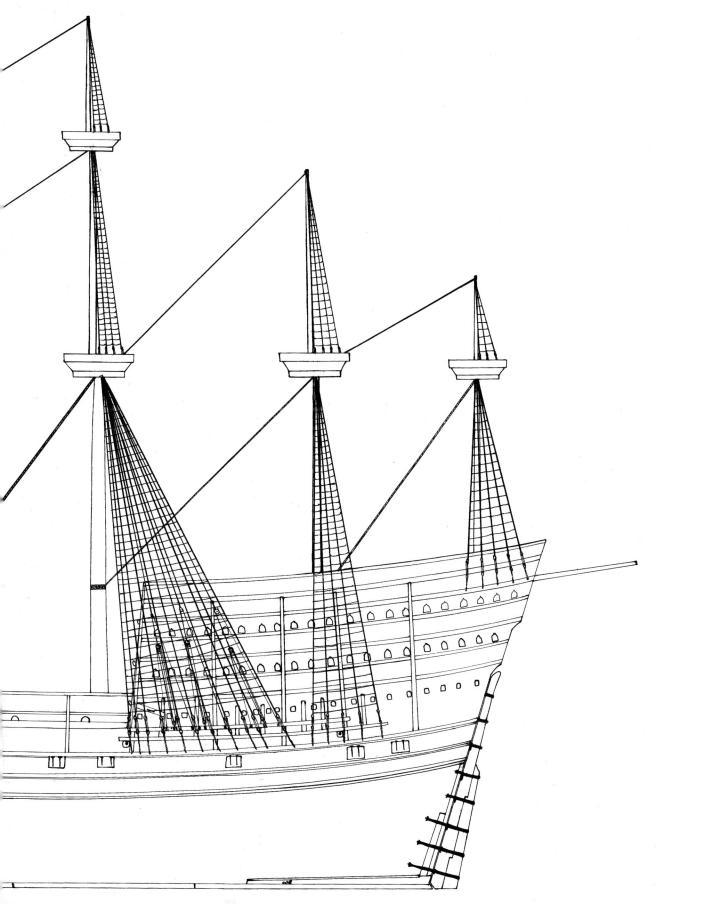

C Masts and yards

C3   Running rigging – sail control (1/192 scale)

C3

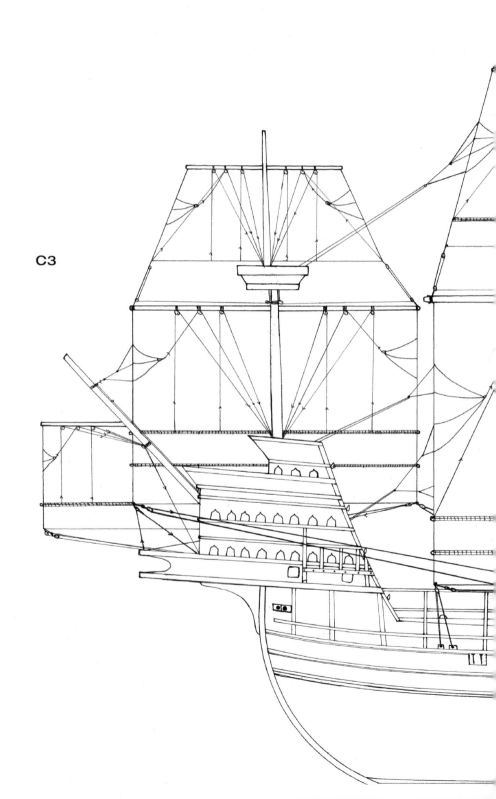

C Masts and yards

C4   Running rigging – yard control (1/192 scale)

C4

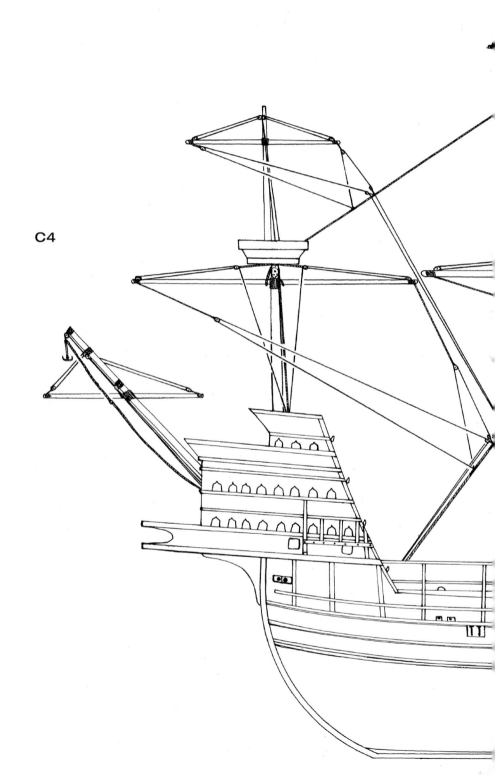

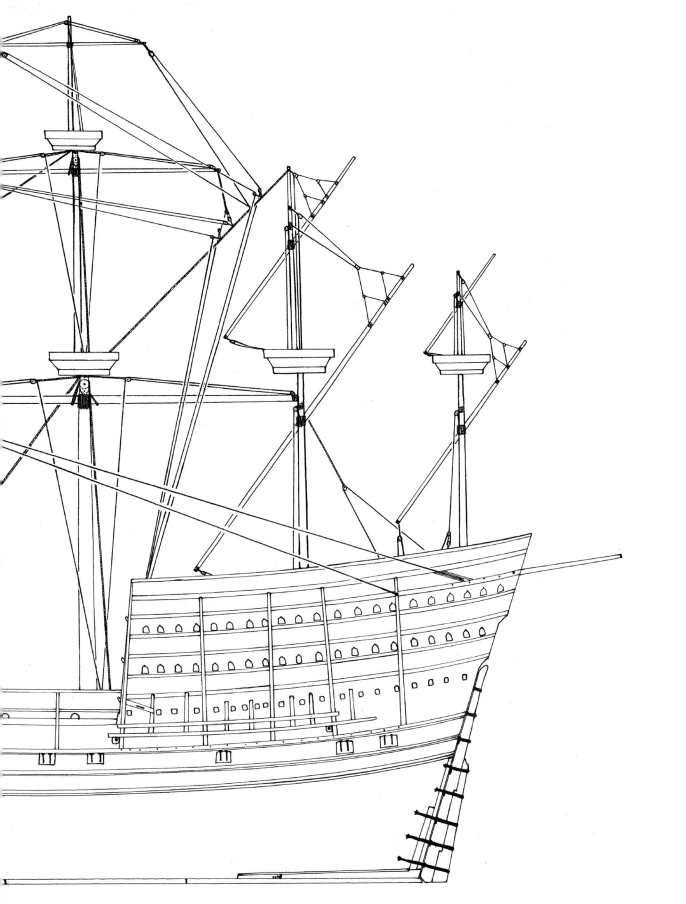

C Masts and yards

C5   **Foremast and fore topmast (1/192 scale)**

1   Foremast
2   Fore topmast
3   Blocks for lifts

C6   **Main mast, main topmast and main topgallant mast (1/192 scale)**

1   Main mast
2   Main topmast
3   Main topgallant mast
4   Sheave
5   Mast step

C7   **Mizzen mast and mizzen topmast (1/192 scale)**

1   Mizzen mast
2   Mizzen topmast
3   Halyard block

C8   **Bonaventure mizzen (1/192 scale)**

C9   **Fighting top (1) (1/192 scale) and nailing detail (2) (no scale)**

1   Top capping
2   Top rim
3   Crosstrees
4   Ribs
5   Mast hole
6   Lower capping
7   Nail

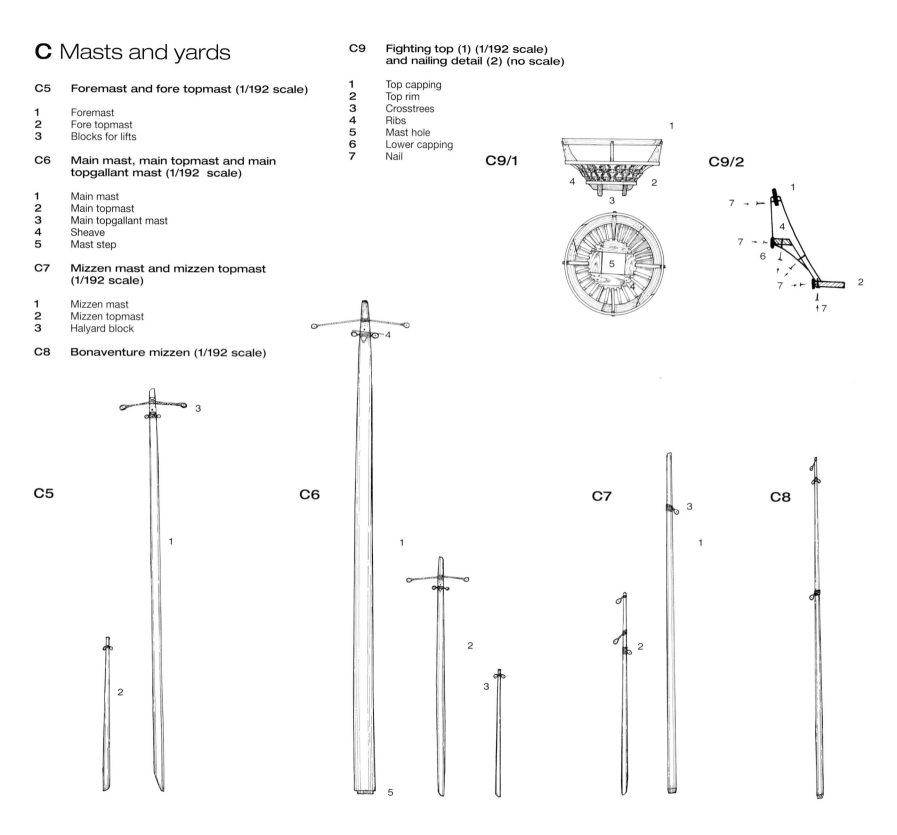

C9/1

C9/2

C5

C6

C7

C8

C10 Bowsprit and yard (1/192 scale)

1 Bowsprit
2 Bowsprit yard
3 Blocks for lifts and halyards

C11 Foreyard and foretop yard (1/192 scale)

1 Foretop yard
2 Foreyard
3 Blocks for lifts
4 Pendants for braces

C12 Main yard, main topyard and main topgallant yard (1/192 scale)

1 Main topgallant yard
2 Main topyard
3 Main yard
4 Woolding
5 Scarf joint
6 Blocks for lifts
7 Pendants for braces

C13 Mizzen yard and mizzen topyard (1/192 scale)

1 Mizzen topyard
2 Mizzen yard
3 Blocks for tacks
4 Eyes for crowsfeet for lifts

C14 Bonaventure mizzen yard and Bonaventure mizzen topyard (1/192 scale)

1 Bonaventure mizzen topyard
2 Bonaventure mizzen yard

C15 Outligger yard (1/192 scale)

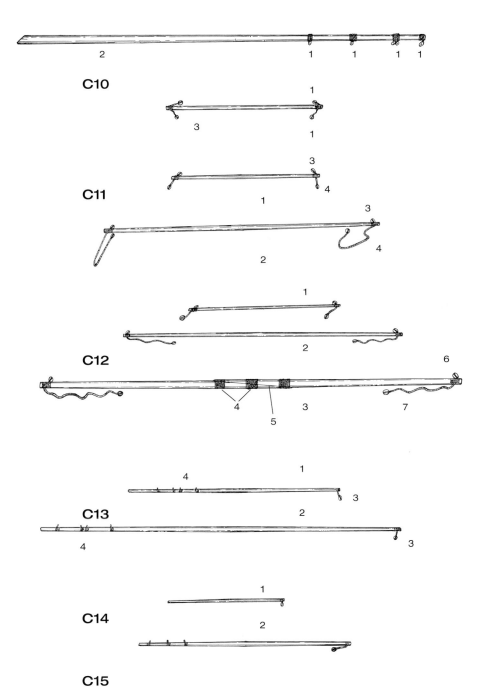

D Sails and sail trimming

D1 **Main course (1) bonnet and (2) drabbler (1/192 scale)**

1 Boltrope
2 Cringles for martinets
3 Cringles for bowlines
4 Eyelets for bonnet

D2 **Main topsail (1) and bonnet (1/192 scale)**

D1

D1/1

D1/2

D2

D2/1

D3 Topgallant sail (1/192 scale)

D4 Martinet (no scale)

1 Sheave
2 Heart block

D5 Bowline (no scale)

1 Heart block

D6 Fore course, (1) bonnet and (2) drabbler (1/192 scale)

D7 Fore topsail (1/192 scale)

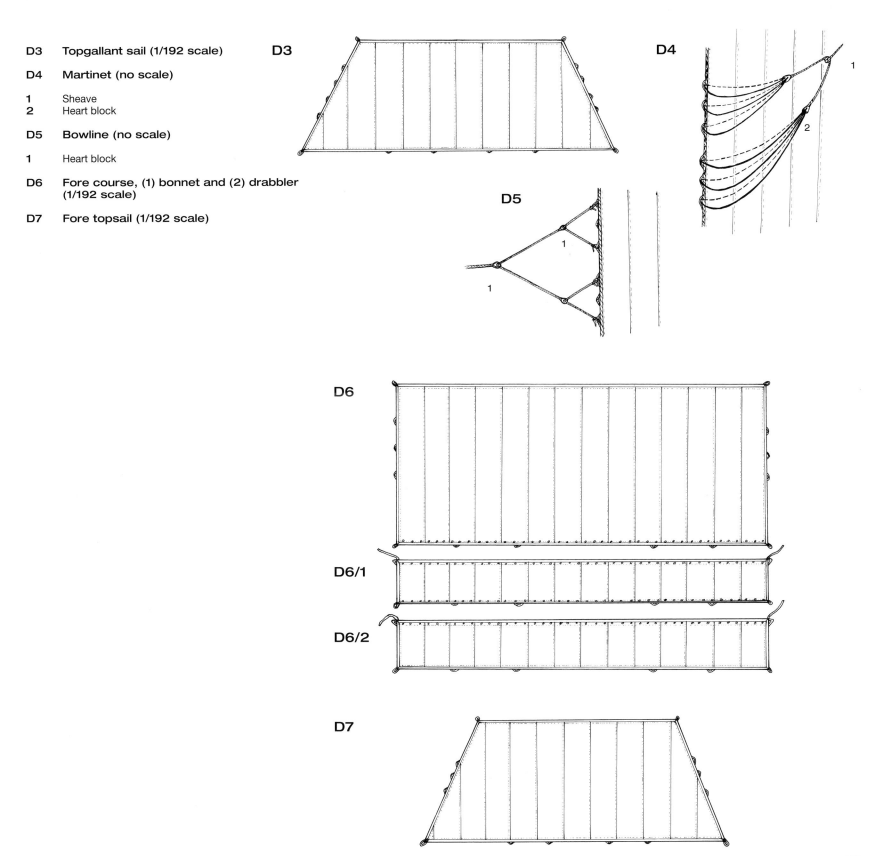

D Sails and sail trimming

D8 Bowsprit sail and (1) bonnet (1/192 scale)

D9 Mizzen sail and (1) mizzen topsail (1/192 scale)

D10 Bonaventure mainsail and (1) topsail (1/192 scale)

D11 Detail of sail's bolt rope and fastening to the yard (no scale)

1 Wedge
2 Robands
3 Yard
4 Cringles
5 Bolt rope
6 Tabling
7 Eye for sheet or tack

D12 Knot for tying the sail to the yard and side view (1) (no scale)

1 Bolt rope
2 Cringle
3 Yard
4 Aft side of sail
5 Fore side of sail

D13 Cringle from the sail recovered from the *Mary Rose* (no scale)

1 Puddenings

D14 Cringle in bolt rope for bowline (no scale)

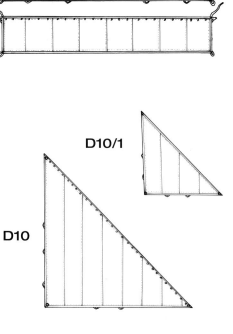

D8

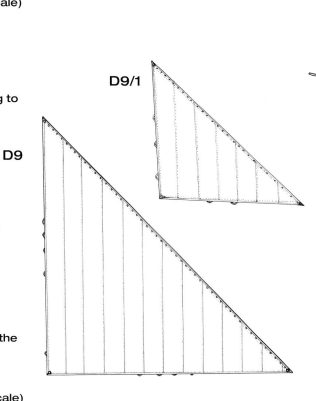

D9/1

D9

D10/1

D10

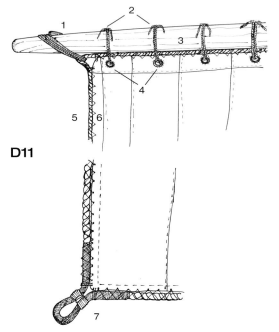

D11

D12

D12/1

D13

D14

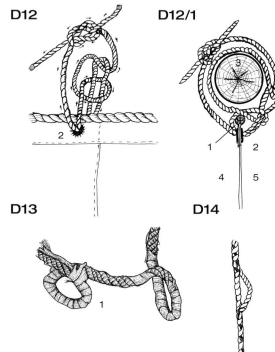

D15 Lacing of bonnets to sails (no scale)

D16 Arrangement of tack, sheet and clew
(no scale)

1 Tack
2 Clew
3 Sheet

D17 Shearhook (no scale)

D18 Shearhook tied to end of the yard
(no scale)

1 Rope woldings
2 Cleat
3 Bolt rope
4 Sheerhook
5 Sail
6 Double sheerhooks

D15/1

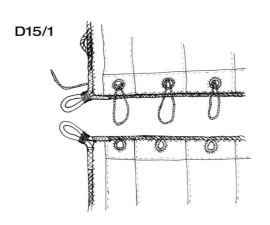

D16

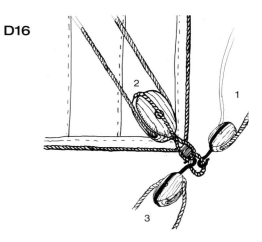

D15/2

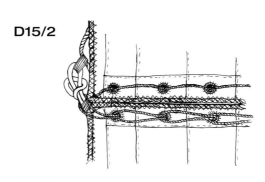

D17

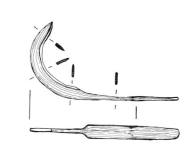

D15/3

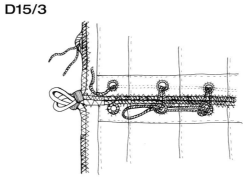

D18

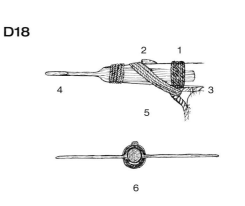

D Sails and sail trimming

D19 Deadeye arrangement (no scale)

1 Deadeye
2 Rigging rail
3 Chainplate
4 Chain
5 Eyebolt
6 Wale

D20 Deadeye and chain (no scale)

1 Deadeye
2 Ring
3 Chain

D21 Deadeyes fore (1) main (2) mizzen (3) and bonaventure (4) masts (1/10 scale)

D19

D20

D21/1

D21/2

D21/3

D21/4

D22   Examples of blocks (1/10 scale)

1   Single block
2   Double block
3   Clew block
4   Heart block
5   Shoe block
6   Snatch block
7   Fiddle block
8   Double clew block
9   Sister block

D23   Main halyard block (1/48 scale)

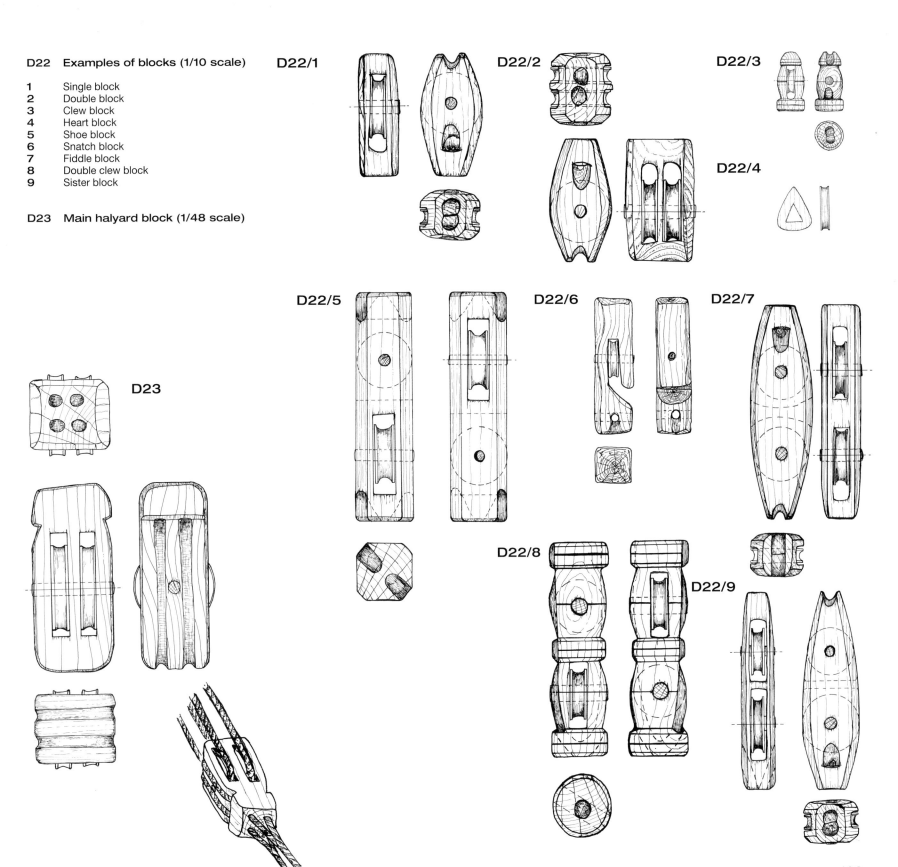

D22/1

D22/2

D22/3

D22/4

D23

D22/5

D22/6

D22/7

D22/8

D22/9

D Sails and sail trimming

D24 Main halyard windlass (1) and side elevation with fastenings (2)

D25 Parrell bead (1) and parrell rib and beads (2) (1/5 scale)

1 Beads
2 Beads and rib (side view)

D26 Parrell rigging diagram

D27 Smaller parrell rib and bead

1 Beads
2 Beads and rib (side view)

D28 Smaller parrell rigging diagram

D24/1   D24/2

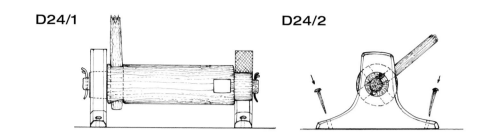

D25/1

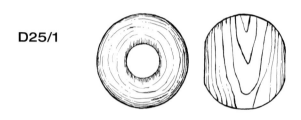

D25/2

1   2

D26

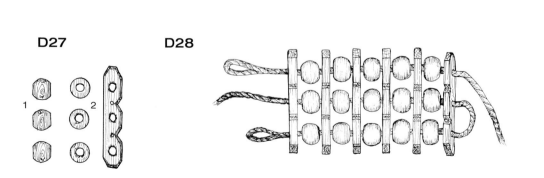

D27   D28

1   2

E Ship's boats

E1 Ship's boat – plan and elevation (1/72 scale)

1 Outer sternpost
2 Inner sternpost
3 Rudder
4 Tiller
5 Sternpost knee
6 Windlass
7 Aft deck
8 Oarlocks
9 Mast step
10 Mast partner
11 Benches
12 Deck
13 Foredeck
14 Sheave at head for lifting
15 Knees

E2 Ship's boat – sail plan (1/96 scale)

1 Halyards
2 Yard
3 Sheet
4 Mast
5 Backstays
6 Parrell
7 Forestay
8 Tack

E3 Ship's boat – detail of masthead (no scale)

1 Masthead sheave for main halyard
2 Backstays
3 Forestay
4 Single block

E4 Ship's boat head with iron band and sheave (no scale)

1 Sheave
2 Anchor rope
3 Iron band
4 Stem
5 Through bolts

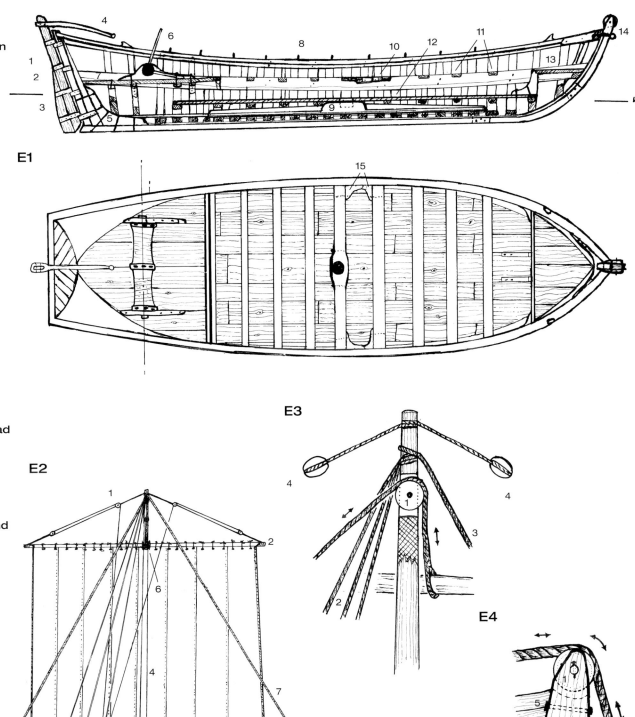

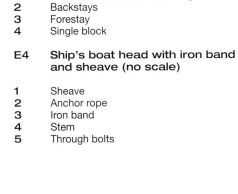

105

E Ship's boats

E5 Cock boat sail plan (1/72 scale)

E6 Cock boat elevation and plan (1/72 scale)

1   Tiller
2   Rudder
3   Sternpost
4   Sternpost knee
5   Aft deck
6   Knees
7   Mast step
8   Mast partner
9   Oarlocks
10 Transom
11 Benches
12 Deck
13 Foredeck

E7 Ship's boat oar 20ft (1) and cock boat oar 16ft (2) (1/48 scale)

E5

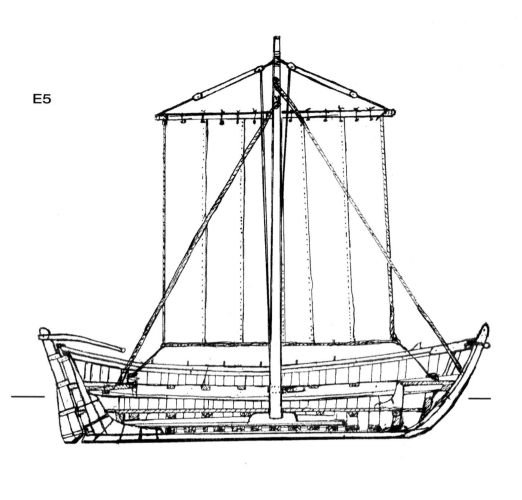

E7/1   E7/2

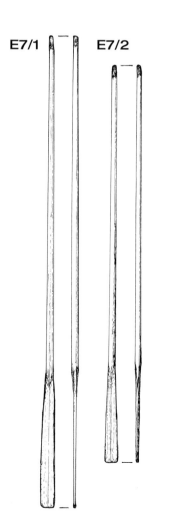

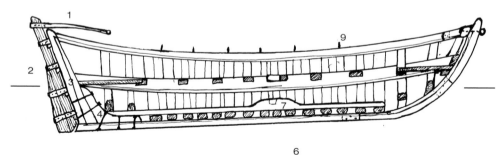

E6

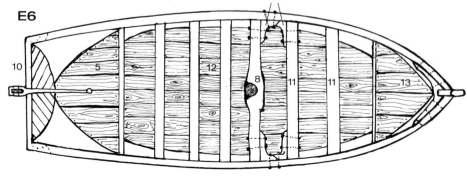

F Anchoring

F1 **Sheet anchor (1/96 scale)**

1 Ring
2 Nut
3 Eye
4 Stock
5 Shank
6 Bell
7 Throat
8 Weald
9 Arm
10 Palm
11 Crown
12 Fluke

F2 **Bowyer anchor (1/96 scale)**

F3 **Kedging anchor (1/96 scale)**

F4 **Dystrelles (1/96 scale)**

F5 **Anchor stock – generic constructional detail (no scale)**

1 Bolt hole
2 Inside face
3 Treenails

F6 **Anchor – generic construction (no scale)**

1 Ring
2 Nut
3 Eye
4 Stock
5 Tenon
6 Mortice for tenon
7 Rebate
8 Shank
9 Wealded scarf joint
10 Palm
11 Crown
12 Fluke
13 Bill
14 Wealded top part

F7 **Anchor – stocked with anchor cable tied to the anchor ring and anchor trip spliced to the crown (no scale)**

F8 **Anchor buoy (1/24 scale)**

F9 **Anchor – knot tied at top and splice at bottom (no scale)**

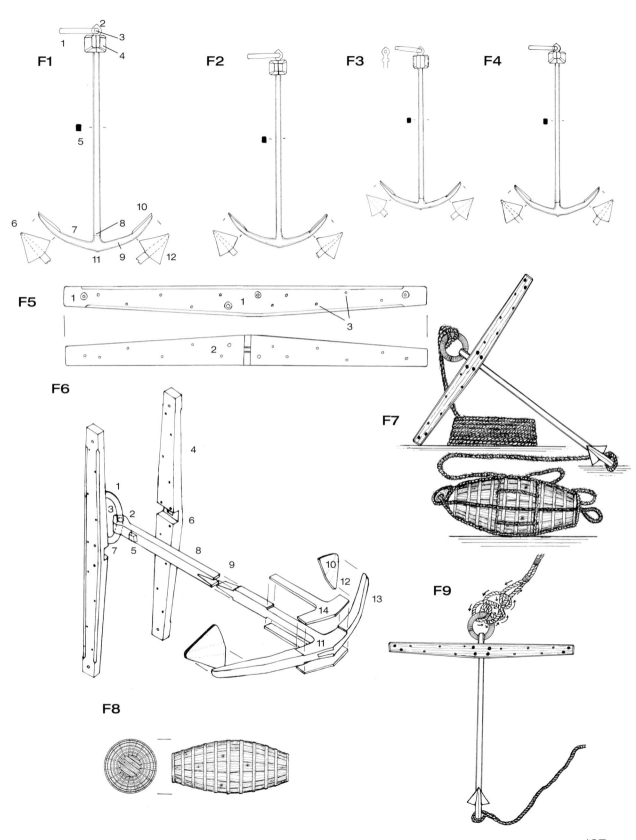

F Anchoring

F10   Grappling hook with chain (no scale)

This was mounted at the end of the bowsprit and used when grappling another vessel.

1   Painter
2   Chain
3   Grapnel

F11   Grappling hook (1/48 scale)

F12   Capstan – plan (1), elevation (2), capstan bar (3) and isometric reconstruction (4) (1/96 scale)

F13   Capstan base (1) section, (2) plan, (3) underside showing rebates for the ledges (1/96 scale)

1   Iron pawls
2   Rebate for ledges

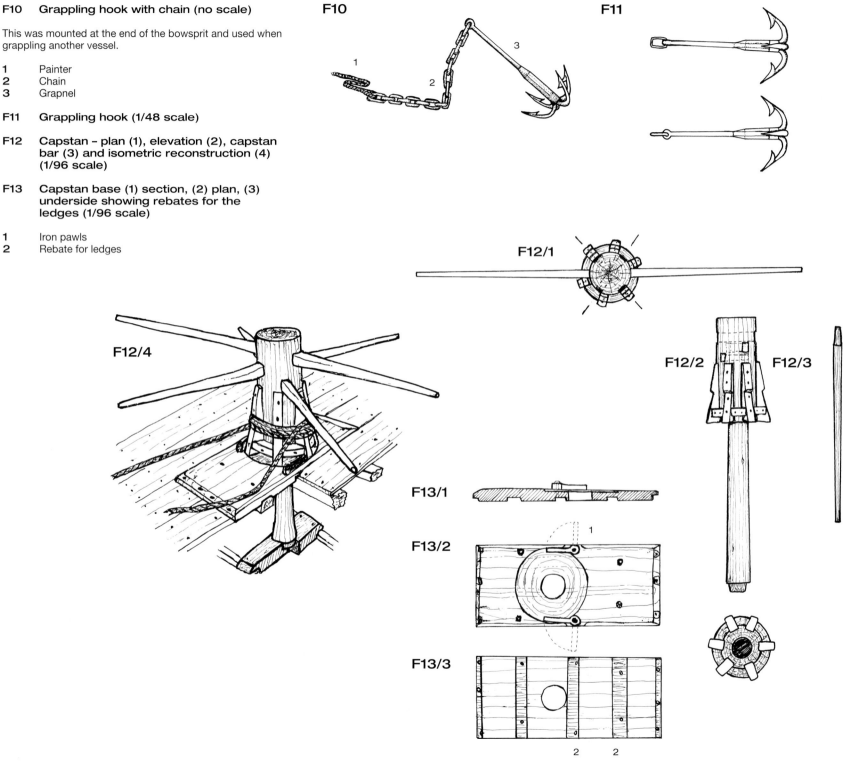

F14 Windlass (1) and side view (2)

F15 Cat davit rigged with hook (no scale)

1 Double sheave
2 Single sheave with cat hook

F15/1 Cat (no scale)

1 Double sheave
2 Iron bands

F15/2 Cat davit plan and elevation (no scale)

F16 Cat hook (1/10 scale)

1 Iron hook
2 Single sheave
3 Eye

F17 Fish hook (1/10 scale)

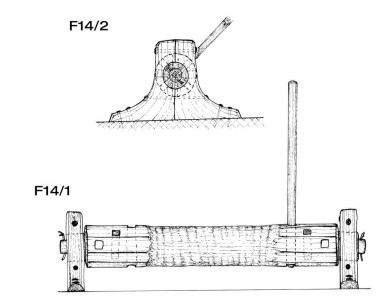

F14/2

F14/1

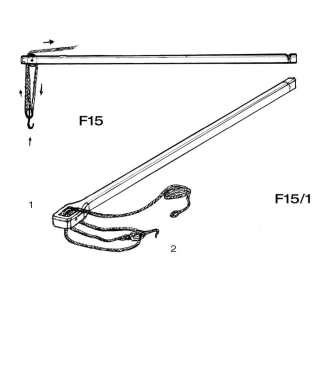

F15

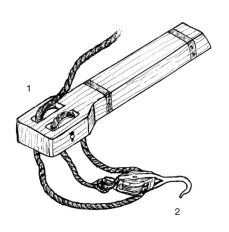

F15/1

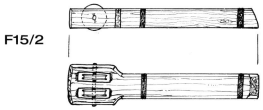

F15/2

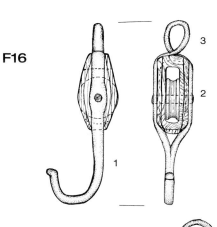

F16

F17

G Habiliments of war c1511

G1   Great curtows (1/72 scale)

G2   Great murders (1/72 scale)

G3   Iron gun stocked with chamber
(1/72 scale)

G4   Sling (1/72 scale)

G1

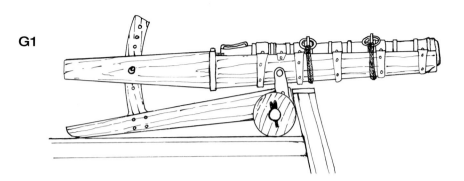

G2

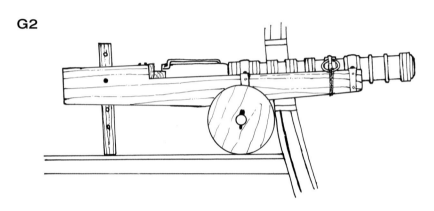

G3

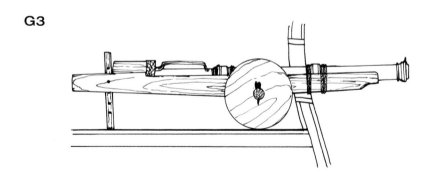

G4

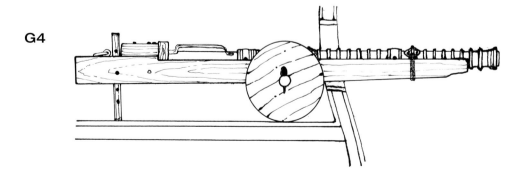

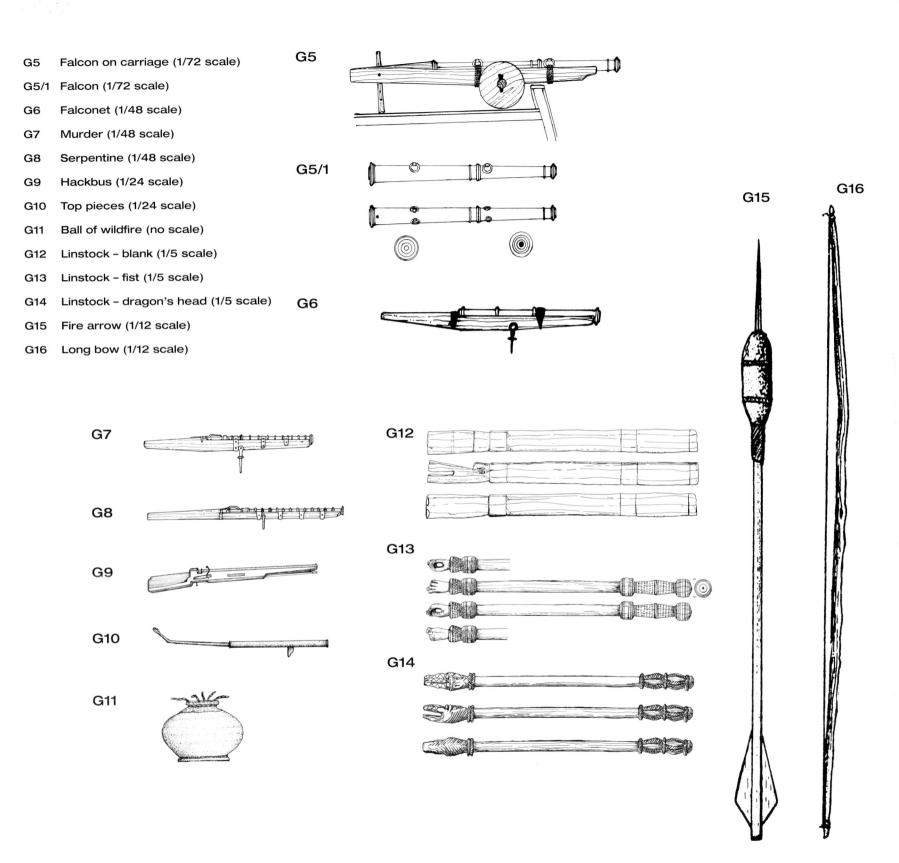

G5 Falcon on carriage (1/72 scale)

G5/1 Falcon (1/72 scale)

G6 Falconet (1/48 scale)

G7 Murder (1/48 scale)

G8 Serpentine (1/48 scale)

G9 Hackbus (1/24 scale)

G10 Top pieces (1/24 scale)

G11 Ball of wildfire (no scale)

G12 Linstock – blank (1/5 scale)

G13 Linstock – fist (1/5 scale)

G14 Linstock – dragon's head (1/5 scale)

G15 Fire arrow (1/12 scale)

G16 Long bow (1/12 scale)

G5

G5/1

G6

G7

G8

G9

G10

G11

G12

G13

G14

G15

G16

G Habiliments of war c1545

GENERIC ORDNANCE ON CARRIAGES

G17   Cannon (1/72 scale)

G18   Culverin (1/72 scale)

G19   Demi-culverin (1/72 scale)

G20   Bastard cannon (1/72 scale)

G21   Cannon royal (1/72 scale)

G22   Port piece (1/72 scale)

G23   Sling – demi-sling – 1/4 sling (1/72 scale)

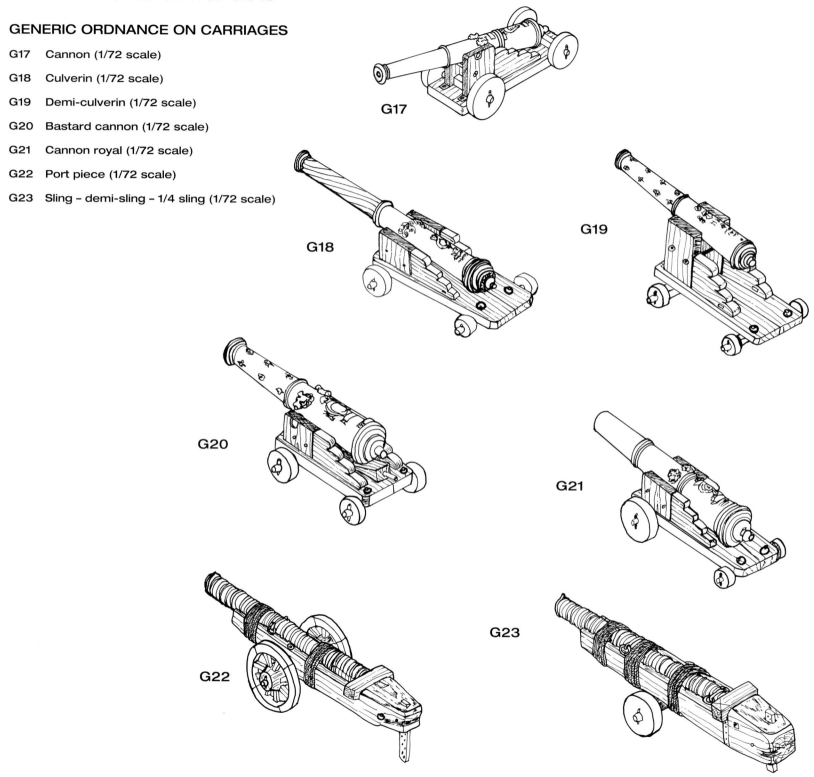

G17

G18

G19

G20

G21

G22

G23

BRASS ORDNANCE

G24   Culverin on carriage

G24/1   Cartouche from culverin (1/5 scale)

G24/2   Detail of cartouche (1/5 scale)

G24/3   Culverin 79A1232 (1/24 scale)

G24/4   Gun carriage for culverin in breast of summercastle (1/24 scale)

G24

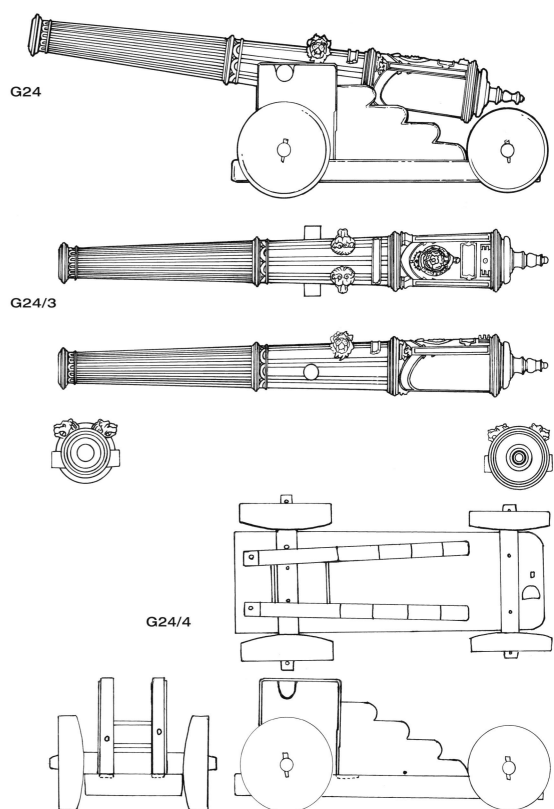

G24/1

G24/3

G24/2

HENRYCVS·OCTAW·DE I·
GRACIA·ANGLIE·ET·FRAN
CIE·REX·FIDEI·DEFENSOR
DNS·HIBERNIE·ET·INTER
RA·SVPREMV·CAPVT·EC
CLESIE·ANGLICANE

ROBERT·AND·JOHN·OWYN·BRETHERYN·BORNE
IN·THE·CYTE·OF·LONDON·THE·SONNES·OF·AN
INGLISSH·MADE·THYS·BASTARD·ANNO·DNI·1537

G24/4

G Habiliments of war c1545

G25   Demi-cannon 81A3000 (1/24 scale)

G26   Demi-cannon 81A3002 (1/24 scale)

G25

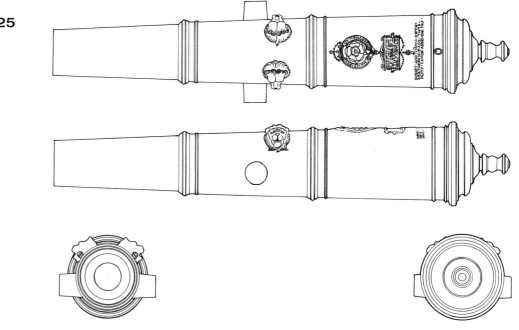

G26

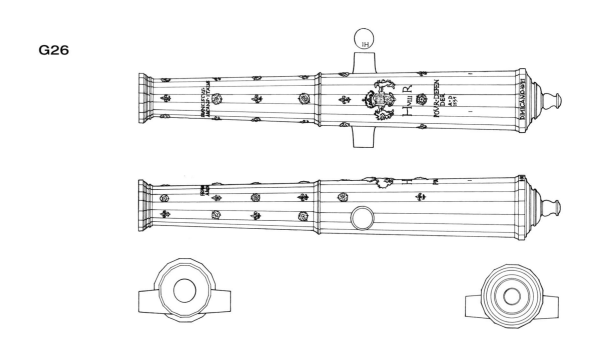

G27

G27   Cannon 81A3003 (1/24 scale)

G28   Cannon royal 79A1276 (1/24 scale)

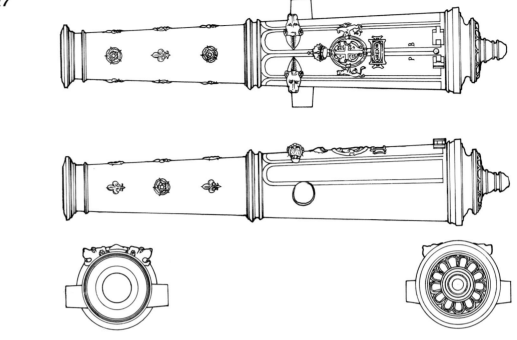

G28

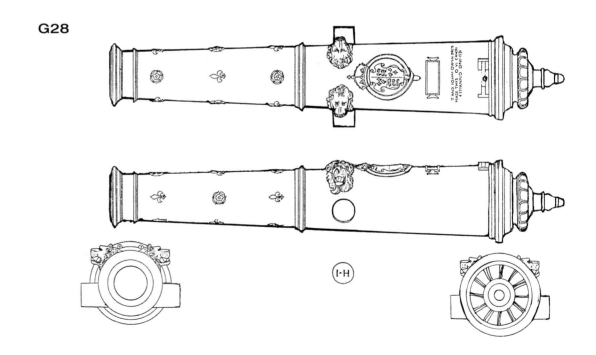

G Habiliments of war c1545

G29   Demi-cannon 79A1277 (1/24 scale)

G30   Culverin 81A1423 (1/24 scale)

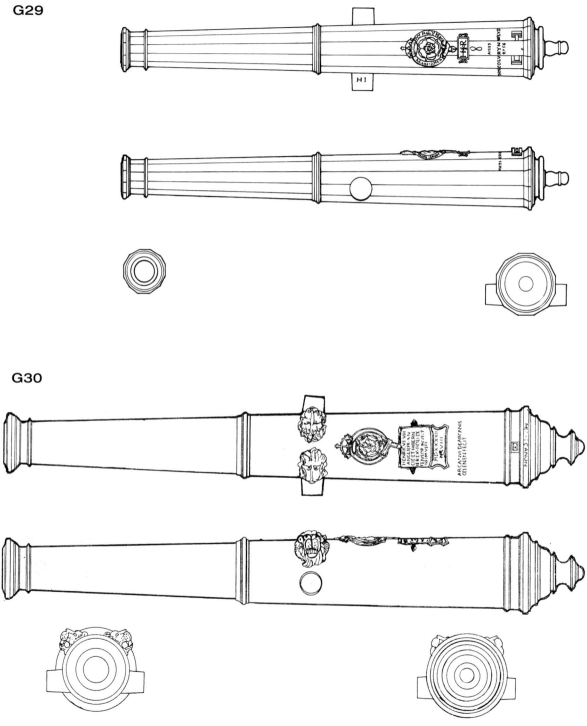

G29

G30

116

G31   Culverin 80A976 (1/24 scale)

G32   Culverin 79A1278 (1/24 scale)

G31

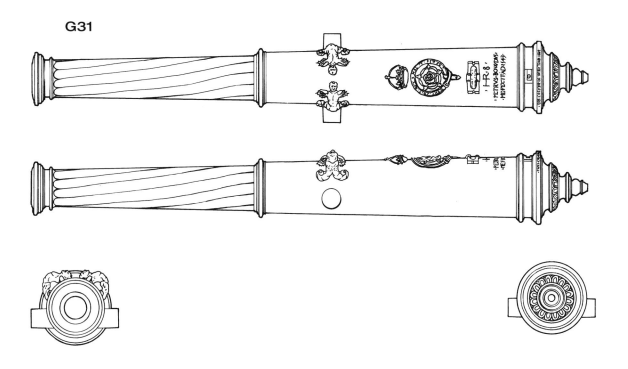

G32

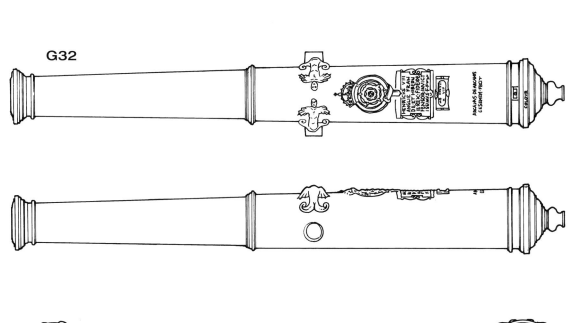

G Habiliments of war c1545

G33   Demi-culverin 79A1279 (1/24 scale)

G34   Minion (1/24 scale)

G33

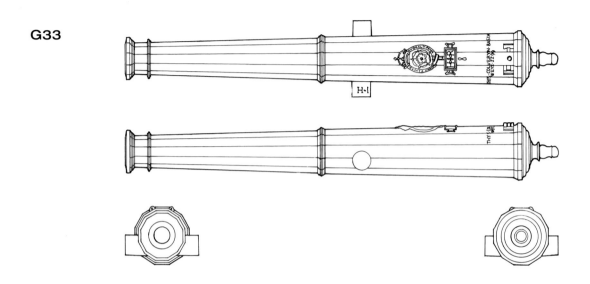

G34

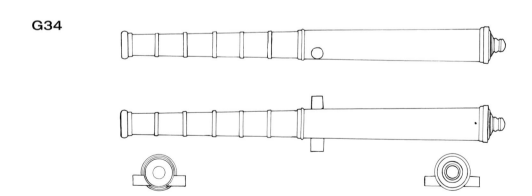

G35   Falcon (1/24 scale)

G35/1   Falcon on carriage (1/24 scale)

G36   Falcon (1/24 scale)

G35

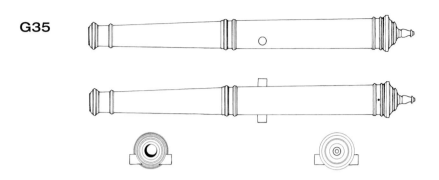

G35/1

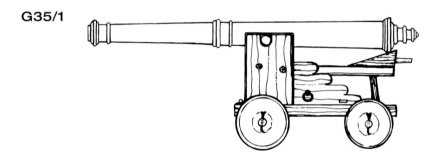

G36

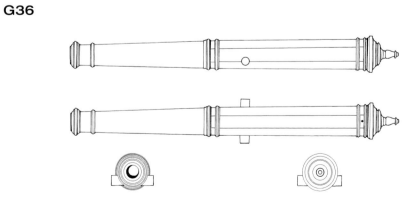

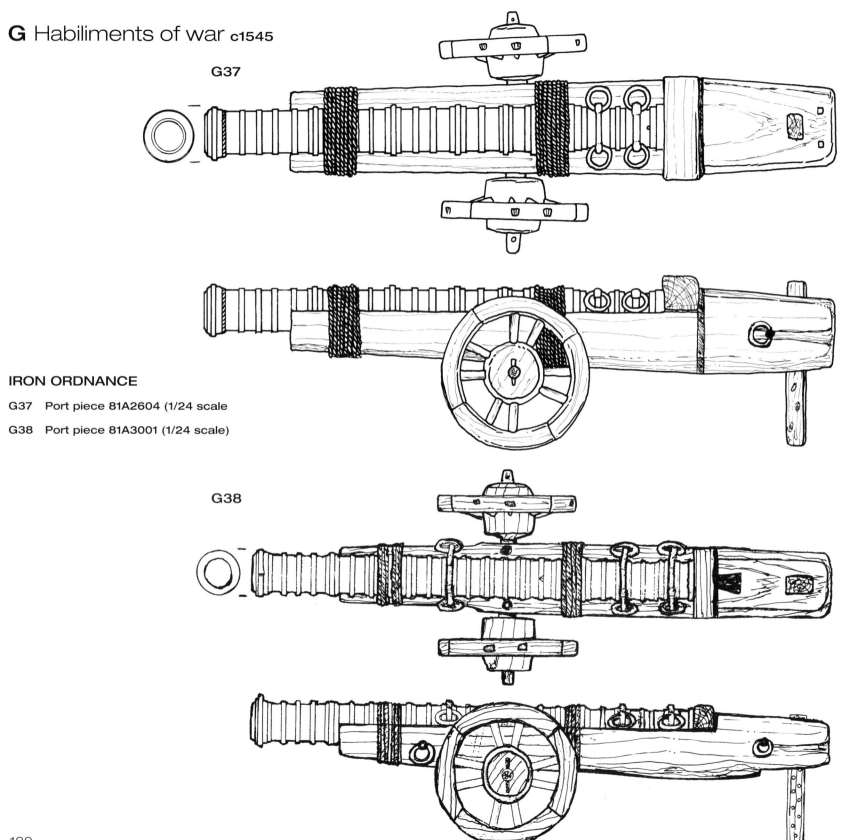

G Habiliments of war c1545

G37

IRON ORDNANCE

G37   Port piece 81A2604 (1/24 scale)

G38   Port piece 81A3001 (1/24 scale)

G38

G39 Demi-sling (1/24 scale)

G40 Sling (1/24 scale)

G39

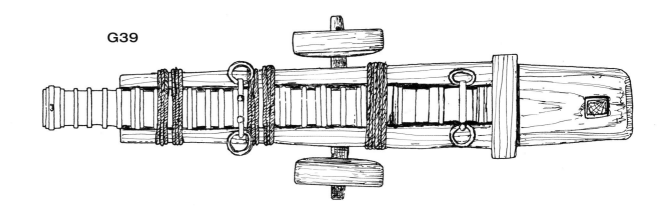

G40

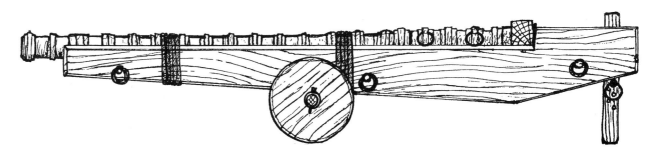

G Habiliments of war c1545

G41   Base (1/24 scale)

G42   Fowler (1/24 scale)

GUN CARRIAGES

G43   Low (1/24 scale)

G43/1 Quion (1/24 scale)

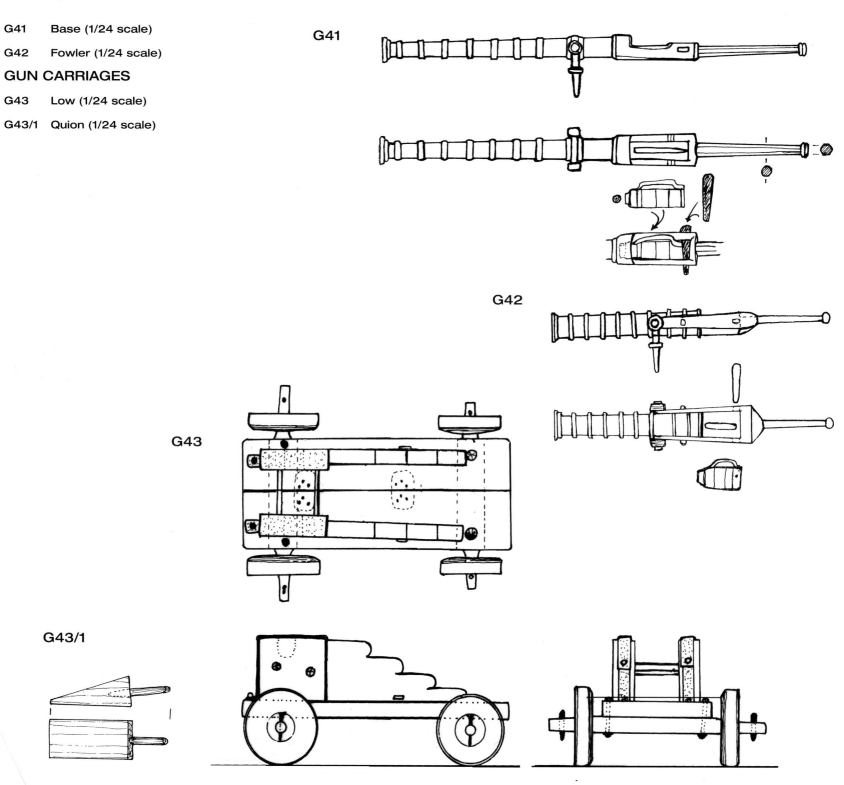

G41

G42

G43

G43/1

G44 Medium (1/24 scale)

G45 High (1/24 scale)

G44

G45

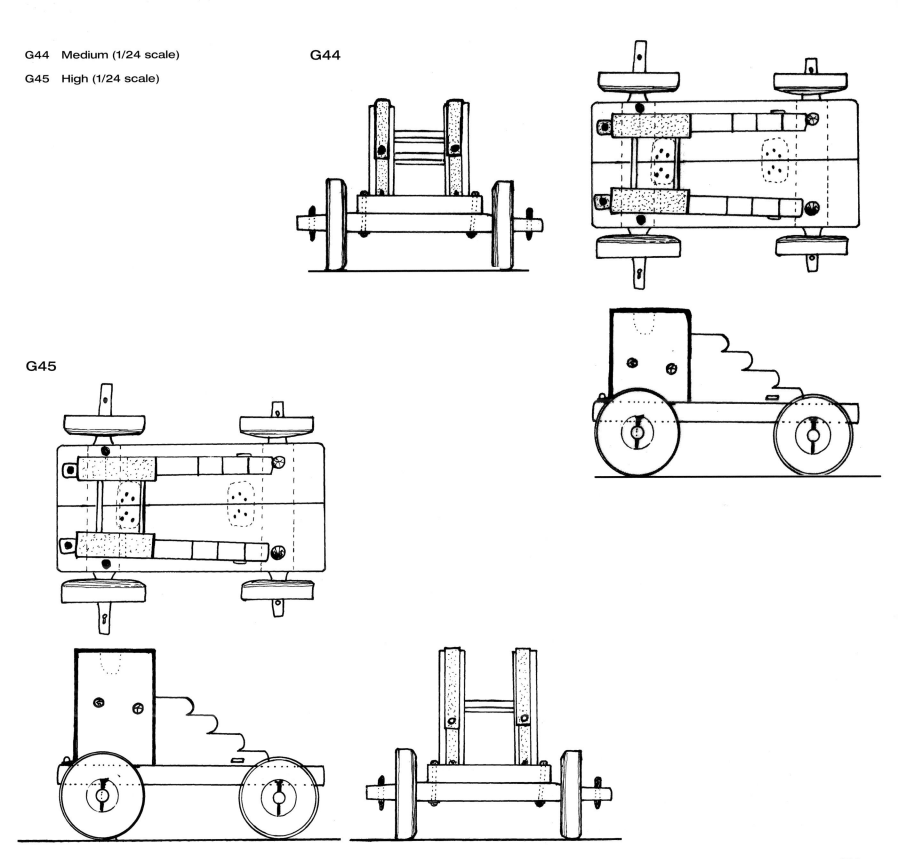

G Habiliments of war c1545

G46   Port piece (1/24 scale)

G47   Sling (1/24 scale)

G46

G47

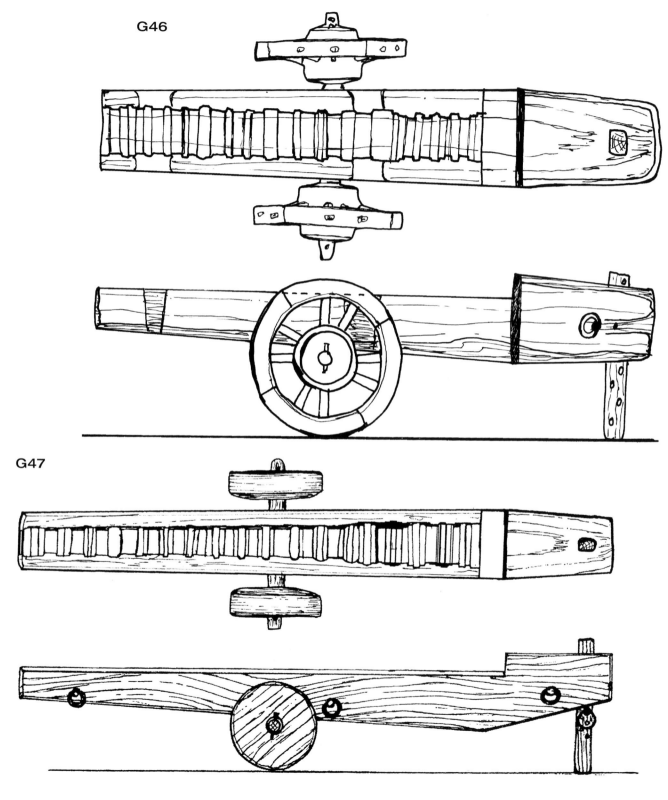

G48   Carriage wheel (1/24 scale)

G49   Elevation leg (1/24 scale)

G50   Breech wedge (1/24 scale)

G51   Wrought iron barrel constructional
       features (1/24 scale)

G52   Breeching rope knot

G53   Breeching for truck carriage

G54   Breeching for wrought carriages

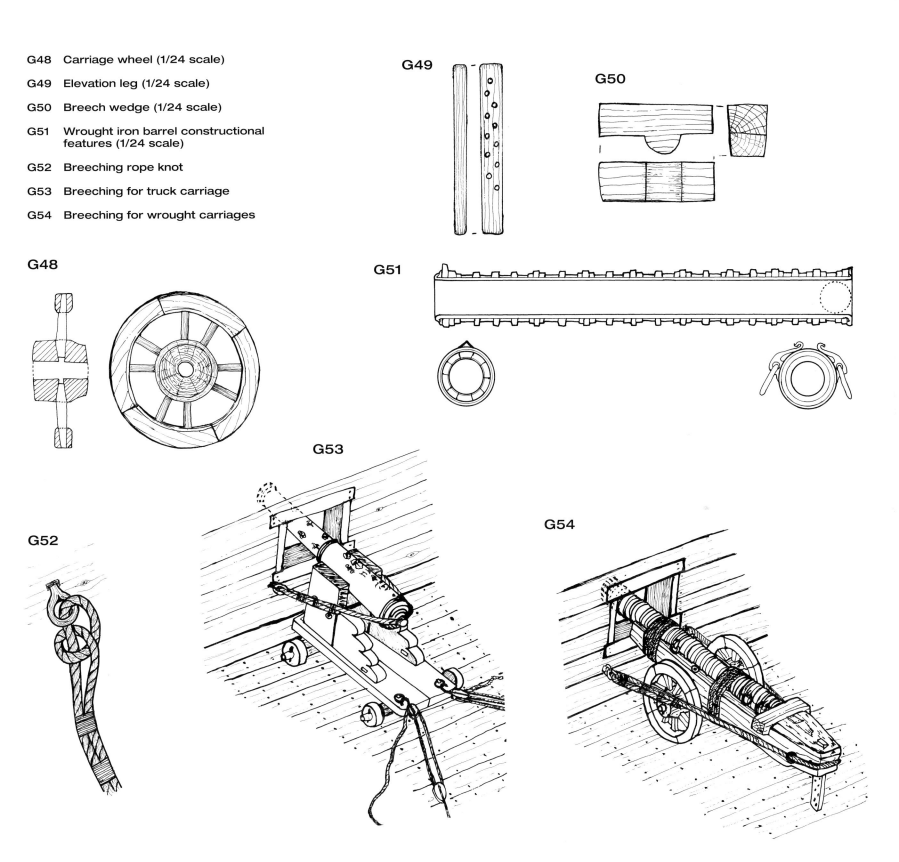

G49

G50

G48

G51

G53

G52

G54

G Habiliments of war c1515–1545

G55   Stone shot (1/24 scale)

G56   Iron shot (1/10 scale)

G57   Bar shot

G58   Star shot

G59   Lead shot/pellets (1/5 scale)

G59/1   Lead shot/pellets mould (1/5 scale)

1   Lead mould tied together ready for pouring lead
2   Mould seam
3   Top of mould
4   Two-part lead shot mould

G60   Canister shot of three types (1/10 scale)

1   Two halves tied together

G61   Dice shot (no scale)

G55

G56

G57

G58

G59

G59/1

G60/1

G60/2

G60/3

G61

MUNITIONS

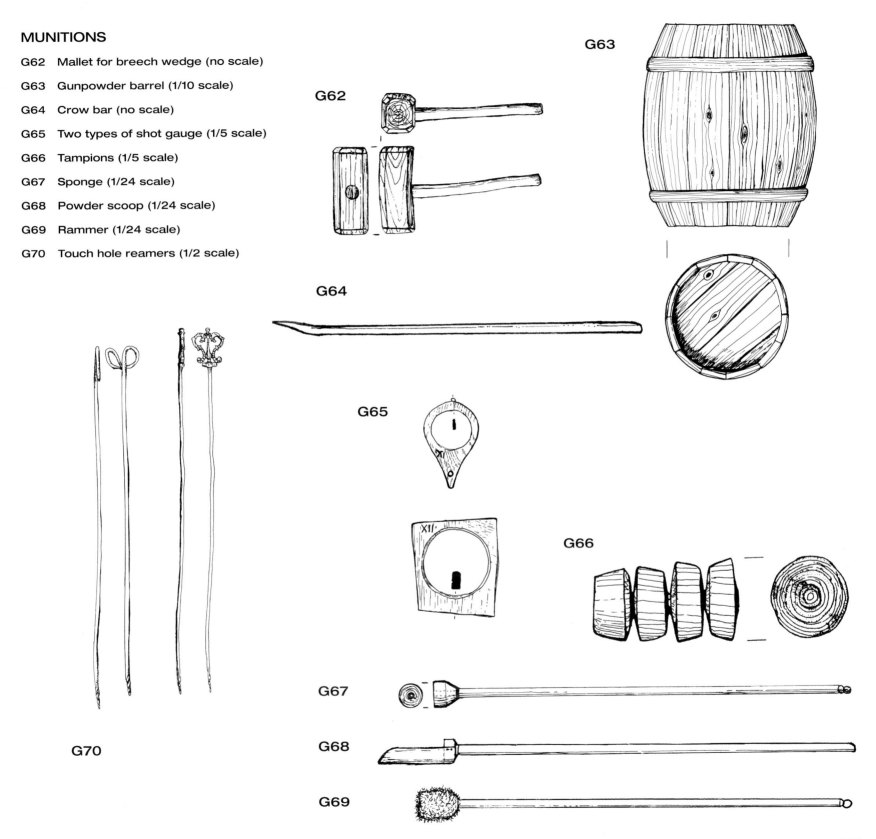

G62

G63

G64

G65

G66

G67

G68

G69

G70

The *Mary Rose* was built in Portsmouth between the summers of 1509 and 1511, and served 34 years in Henry VIII's navy before sinking a few miles off Portsmouth on 19 July 1545. Finding, excavating and raising the *Mary Rose* was the boyhood dream of Alexander McKee, a dream he realised when she was raised on 11 October 1982.

Mac's marauders

From the 1960s McKee, or 'Mac' as he was affectionately known, led a team of enthusiastic volunteer divers on a quest to find the lost remains of the *Mary Rose* in the guise of operation 'Solent ships' (McKee 1982, p46). After a number of dives on the site of the *Royal George* to understand the seabed topography, and after seeing a chart marking the last known resting place of the *Mary Rose*, in May 1966 McKee and his divers unknowingly swam over the *Mary Rose* but saw nothing except a possible scour pit (McKee 1982, p55, 57–58). Between the years of 1966 and 1968 McKee, using the latest in underwater magnetic, side scan and sub-bottom profiling equipment, surveyed the general area of the site but unfortunately it was still covered (McKee 1982, p55–66). However, he was to see his *Mary Rose* for the first time in the acoustic image of the sub-bottom profile of the hidden ship. It was discernible if a bit hazy, like the ultrasonic image of a baby in its mother's womb (Fig 101). With the chart that showed the last known resting place of the *Mary Rose,* McKee was able to cross-reference all his data and find out that this time 'X' did mark the spot (Fig 102). Digging down through the heavy silt and mud of the Solent, the first timbers to be seen were the degraded tops of frames from the port quarter.

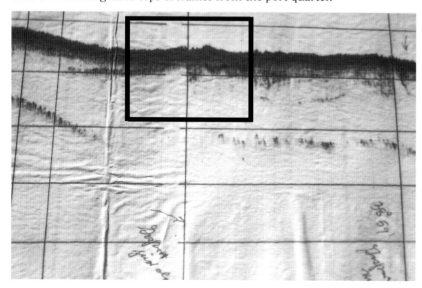

Fig 101 Sub-bottom profile image of *Mary Rose.*

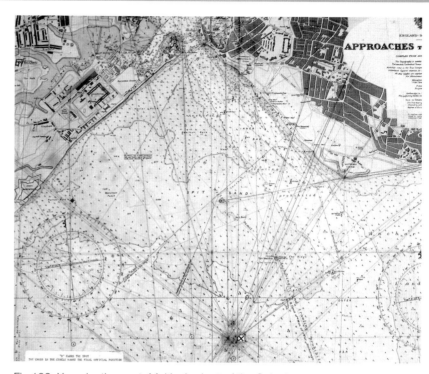

Fig 102 X marks the spot, McKee's chart of the Solent.

From then on, under the archaeological direction of Margaret Rule, McKee carefully and systematically investigated the ship. Starting with these three frames and working until 1978, he and his team revealed the extent of the ship and ascertained that she lay over on her starboard side at about 60 degrees. He then stepped aside, realising that the baby he had nursed had grown up and now had to reach maturity. In 1979 the fateful decision was made to raise the hull of the *Mary Rose* (McKee 1982, p116), and the Mary Rose Trust was set up to do so.

The Mary Rose Trust

Between 1979 and 1982 the newly formed Mary Rose Trust spent £2.8 million on the excavation, salvage and recovery of the *Mary Rose*. This figure does not include the extensive gifts of equipment, time and expertise generously provided by many companies and organisations during this period; nor does it include the costs of operations prior to 1979 (Annual Reports, Mary Rose Trust, 1979–1982). Many skills and techniques were developed during this period, varying from diver management to excavating, surveying, raising, conserving and documenting finds. Some 28,000 dives were carried out between 1979 and 1982 involving over 500 divers, most of them volunteers. The excavation and salvage raised public awareness of our

Fig 103 Raising the *Mary Rose*.

maritime heritage. Most adults in the UK are able to remember the day the *Mary Rose* was raised (Fig 103) and 60 million viewers worldwide saw the first ever live outside broadcast from underwater.

Since 1982 a further £25 million has been spent on recording, publishing and conserving the hull and artefacts recovered (Annual Reports, Mary Rose Trust, 1983–2004). Much of this has been through generous donations, sponsorship and grants from the Heritage Lottery Fund; and much is paid for by the continued support of the visiting and paying public (Annual Reports, Mary Rose Trust, 2005). This has allowed the Trust to carry out important and world-leading research into the methods of both passive and active conservation of the hull and its artefacts, which is available for the

benefit of future projects (Jones). 'Inspiring learning for all' is at the core of the Trust's objectives and encompasses all levels of primary and secondary education, to further education and public education.

Completed in 1511, the career of the *Mary Rose* spans nearly the whole period of Henry VIII's reign. It was a reign that saw dramatic changes in English history with not an inconsiderable impact on British history and subsequently world history. The *Mary Rose* is often called a 'time-capsule' or 'England's Pompey' because of its exceptional collection of over 19,000 artefacts. These span the simple and mundane objects of everyday life to those directly linked to the King himself (Gardiner and Allen, 2005). All of the artefacts come from that fateful day in 1545.

Fig 104 The author underwater recording the stem of the *Mary Rose*, 2004.

More recently (2003–2005) the Mary Rose Trust was funded by the Ministry of Defence to carry out investigations into the archaeological deposits left on the site, most specifically those of the bow and forecastle. These investigations culminated in the recovery of artefacts including another anchor and breech blocks (hinting at heavy guns in the forecastle) but more significantly the remains of port-side timbers and the near complete stem post (Fig 104). The raising of the stempost has meant for the first time there is a full and proper understanding of the bow structure, thus allowing the hull shape of the *Mary Rose* to be reconstructed with 100 per cent confidence.

Significance of the *Mary Rose*

The *Mary Rose* dates from a pivotal period in the development of ship construction and design. The design of the *Mary Rose* was 'revolutionary'; utilising carvel construction, a transom stern and lidded gunports in one vessel, allowing heavy guns to be placed low down in the hull on a single continuous covered gun deck for the first time. As no detailed plans or drawings of ships exist until the late 17th century, the majority of our knowledge of shipbuilding in earlier periods comes from their archaeological remains or iconography. Almost everything about the hull of the *Mary Rose* has increased our knowledge of ships and shipbuilding before, during and after the Tudor period. Initial observations and conclusions are available and are referenced throughout this publication.

The current corpus of archaeological information was finally been published in 2011. This book draws upon the author's intimate knowledge of the ship and collection, as well as published archaeological information in conjunction with contemporary documentary and iconographic sources. As such this presents the current most reliable interpretation of the ship that was the *Mary Rose* as depicted by Anthony Anthony.

The *Mary Rose* today

The *Mary Rose* and her conserved artefacts are now housed under one roof in a purpose-built museum, just a few hundred metres from where she was built. The new museum houses the ship itself, all the conserved artefacts and acts as an educational facility and special venue for social occasions. The building of the new museum was a 20th century undertaking comparable in complexity to the building of the new ship back in 1510 to 1511. It not only had to provide a safe and stable environment for the visitors but also for the ship and artefacts themselves. The strict planning and heritage regulations of working in a historic dockyard (the museum is built over a wet dock) yards from the symbol of the navy's greatest victory (*HMS Victory* herself) also had to be met. In addition, £14 million of the £35 million required to build the museum had to be found from sponsors (Burton). Fortunately, many consider the *Mary Rose* a national treasure worthy of their support and made generous donations.

The vision for the new museum is to tell the story of the *Mary Rose* and her crew. It is this human aspect that brings home the tragedy when she sank in 1545, and also the you and me element of people past. That is what archaeology is about, the evidence of the day-to-day people not just the kings, queens and politicians of history. It is this story that the *Mary Rose* museum excels at; bringing to life the people and conditions on board. Questions as to what people wore, ate, cooked with, games they played and how they made certain objects like the rigging blocks can all be answered and illustrated. While considered a warship and part of the navy, the ship and its crew represents a cross selection of society at that time. It is this that gives the *Mary Rose* significance and contemporary relevance.

The careful recording underwater of each artefact has allowed its story to be told. A simple wooden ruler on its own becomes part of the carpenter's toolbox, alongside its owner the ship's carpenter himself in his cabin. The remains of a dog found by the same cabin, no doubt his companion. A single leather bracer, worn by archers to protect their forearm from the bow's string when it is loosed, on its own does not give us the whole picture. Displayed with the remains and reconstruction of an archer, context and meaning is given to this important part of the fighting machine. In the hold near the kitchen the skeleton of a strong man who had suffered head wounds, a fractured rib and left foot was found. His posture, hinted by evidence from his ribs and back bone, was stooped. This could be a cook,

Fig 105 The stunning new museum building.

maybe even the owner of the wooden bow, with 'Ny Coep Cook' cut into it and the jug with an incised 'Ny Cop', possibly employed on lighter duties for armed services previously rendered to the crown. An individual thimble-ring could be considered a woman's possession. It was, however, found within the jerkin of a man, along with a powder flask top, who was by the main deck companionway leading out of the ship. His jerkin had once supported the cross of St George, as seen on contemporary illustrations at the time. No doubt this is one of the gunners vainly attempting to escape the sinking ship, his thimble once used to sew together the cloth gunpowder carriages trapped with him.

Seeing the *Mary Rose*

The Mary Rose Trust is not a government-sponsored museum and therefore survives on its continued ability to attract the support of the public. Why though does the *Mary Rose* attract such support and enquiry? A visit to the Trust's new museum in Portsmouth Historic Dockyard to see the ship and artefacts will allow the reader to answer this question for themselves, and acknowledge that the *Mary Rose* and her collection is a priceless and valuable part of our national heritage. For opening times and travel guide, please visit the Trust's website at www.maryrose.org or Tel: +44 (0)23 9281 2931.

References

Burton, A, *The Mary Rose Museum - The Story continues…*, Stroud, 2014

Jones, AM, *For Future Generations: Conservation of a Tudor Maritime Collection*, The Archaeology of the *Mary Rose*: Vol V, Mary Rose Trust, 2003

McKee, A, *How We Found the Mary Rose*, Souvenir Press, 1982

Fig 107 *Mary Rose* decks.

Fig 106 *Mary Rose* in the museum looking from the stern.

Fig 108 *Mary Rose* in the museum looking into the hold.

The significance of the *Mary Rose* is more than the ship herself. While the ship is a unique Tudor warship and gives us an insight into ship design and building at the end of the medieval period, there is more to her archaeology than that. Her armaments are a window into an active warship at the birth of the broadside supremacy. The guns themselves represent some of the earliest ordnance from the fledgling English ordnance industry. Among the armament, and unique in the world, are the cast iron hailshot pieces (see page 35), shield guns (Fig 109) and longbows (Fig 111). The longbow collection has allowed archaeologists and historians to have physical specimens to record and interpret, but as so many survive to also test a few to destruction. More unique then the longbows is the single horn

Fig 109 Shield guns.

Fig 110 Truck carriage and gun.

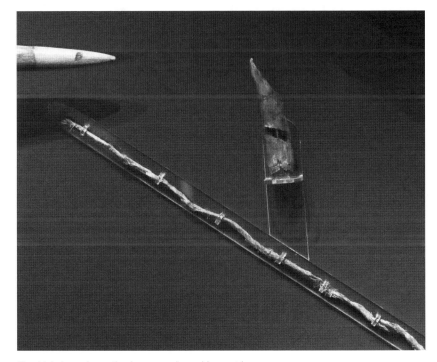

Fig 111 Longbow tip, horn nock and bowstring.

Fig 112 Gun deck reconstruction in the museum.

nock (Fig 111) which would have fitted to one end of a bow. This find only survived as it was encased in a concretion. The partial remains of a single bowstring were recovered in the more recent excavations (Fig 111) completing the bow. The longbow combined with the archer himself, his brace, quiver of arrows and leather jerkin is unique in the world. Nowhere else can you see the complete assemblage of the Great War bow and archer upon which the great English victories of Crécy and Agincourt were founded (see page 36).

Other unique finds include parts of the navigational equipment such as the earliest English ship's log. An instrument for telling the speed of the ship through the water. The *Mary Rose* example predates its supposed introduction in the 1590s. The ship's gimbled compass and tide gauge were only just being referred to in historical texts. To entertain the officers a Tudor quartet was on board (Fig 118), including a person who played the still shame or Douçaine. While known from historical sources the

Fig 113 Detail of a bronze gun.

Fig 114 Tudor quill and ink holder.

Fig 115 *Mary Rose* sand glasses.

Mary Rose example is unique in the world. The mundane Tudor bricks of the oven might not be unique in themselves, but nowhere else can you see an original Tudor furnace along with its cauldron (see page 42). The same can be said of the strange and unusual moneylender's purse. So unusual is it that until recently it had not been properly identified (Fig 116). Taken as a whole the *Mary Rose* and her artefacts are a unique collection and step back in time to the Tudor period.

Fig 116 Moneylender's purse.

Fig 118 Musical instruments from the *Mary Rose*.

Fig 117 Stools and wooden jugs.

H Archaeological drawings

H1   The archaeological remains of the *Mary Rose* as recorded
        in the ship hall (1/192 scale)

H2   The archaeological remains of the *Mary Rose*
        superimposed over the Anthony Roll reconstruction of the
        ship (1/192 scale)

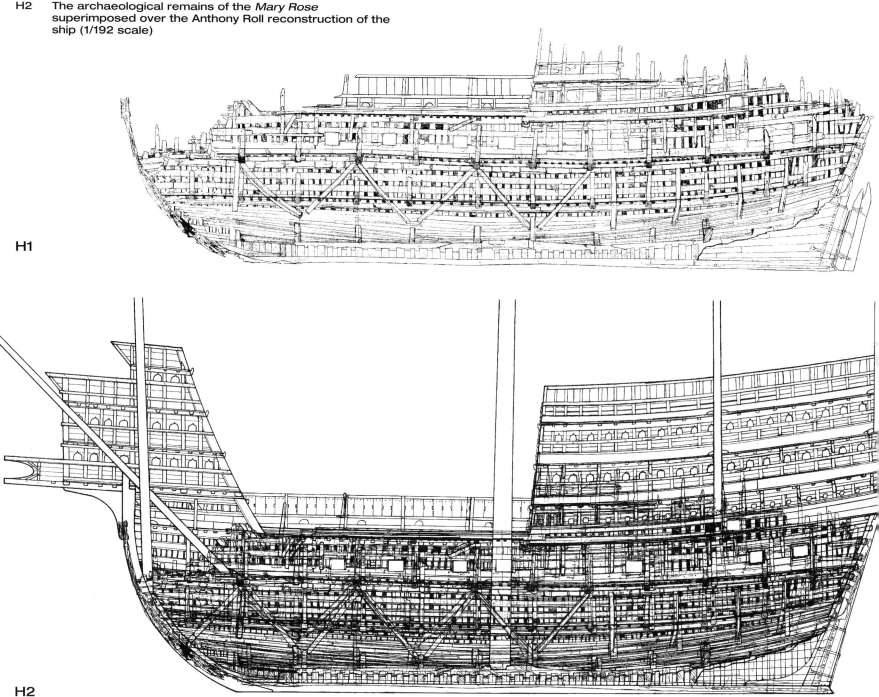

H1

H2

SECTIONS AT THE BEAMS (1/192 scale)

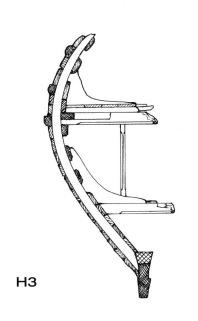

H3

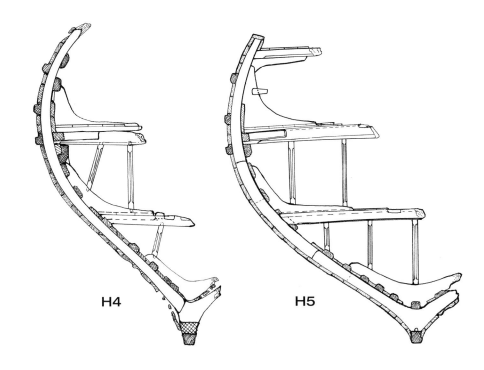

H4

H5

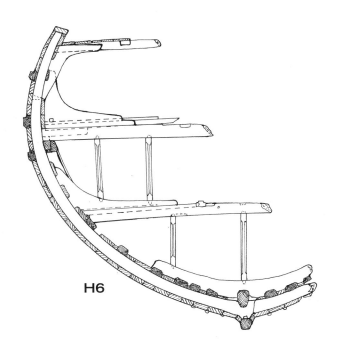

H6

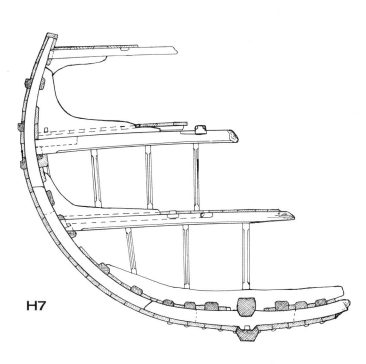

H7

H Archaeological drawings

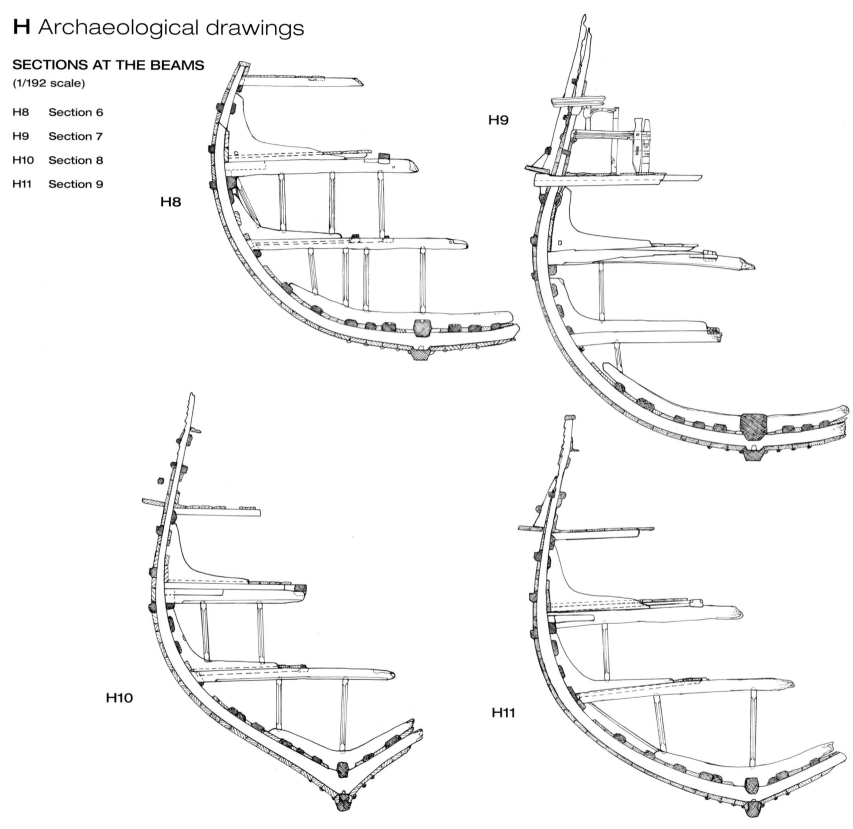

H8

H9

H10

H11

SECTIONS AT THE BEAMS

(1/192 scale)

H12   Section 10

H13   Section 11

H14   Section 12

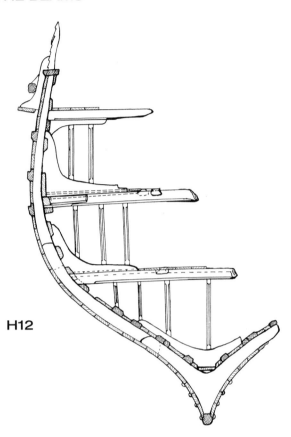

H12

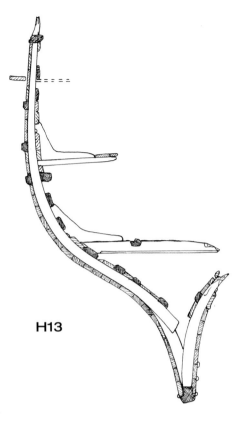

H13

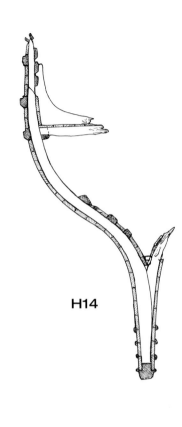

H14

H15   Roman numerals inscribed into the
       beams of each section (no scale)

H15

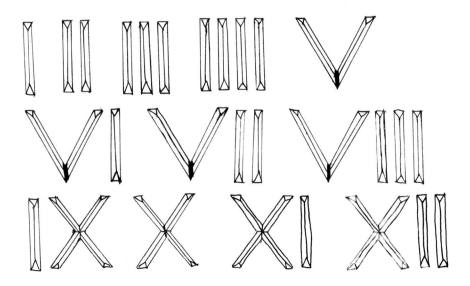

H Archaeological drawings

H16 Internal constructional
elevation of ship as found
(1/96 scale)

H17 Internal constructional
elevation of ship in the
museum (1/192 scale)

H18 External constructional
elevation of ship in the
museum (1/192 scale)

H16

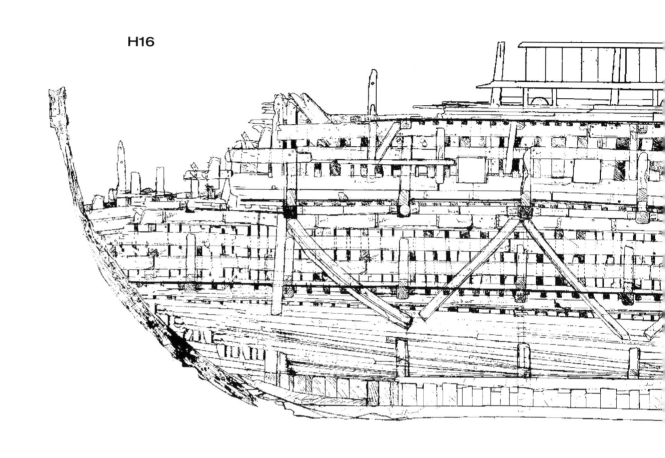

H17

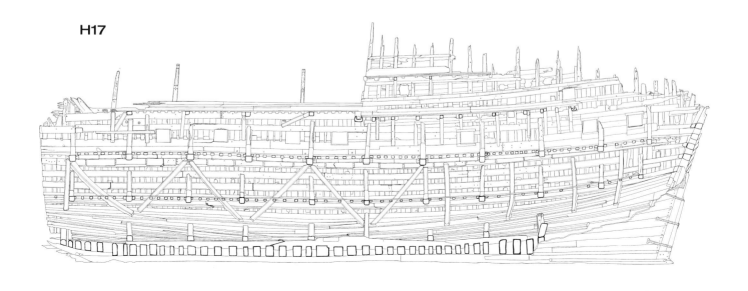

H18

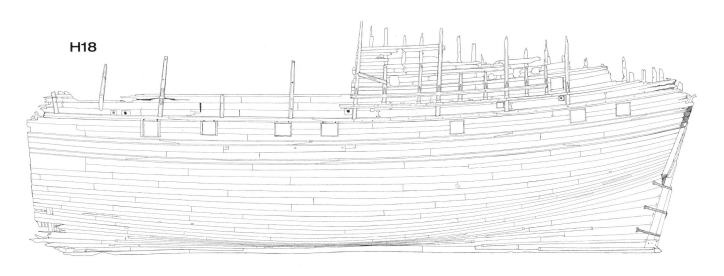

H Archaeological drawings

H19   Hold (1/192 scale)

H20   False orlop deck beams
           (1) and planked (2)
           (1/192 scale)

H21   Main orlop deck beams
           (1) and planked (2)
           (1/192 scale)

H19

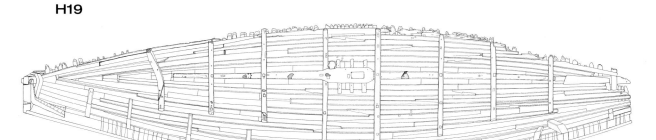

H20/1

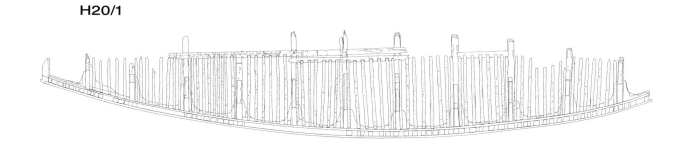

H20/2

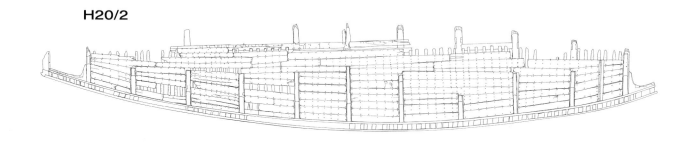

H21/1

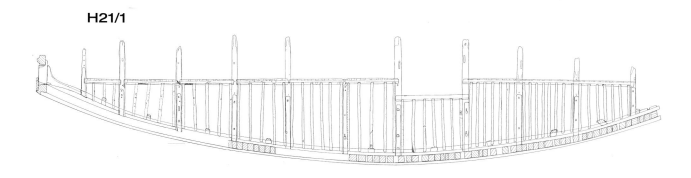

H22 Forecastle nether deck, waist, nether deck of the summer castle beams (1) and planked (2) (1/192 scale)

H23 Stern elevation of ship as found (1/192 scale)

H24 Summercastle deck beams (1) and planked (2) (1/192 scale)

H21/2

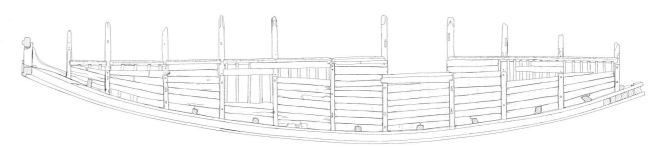

H22/1

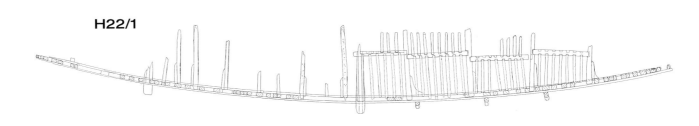

H22/2

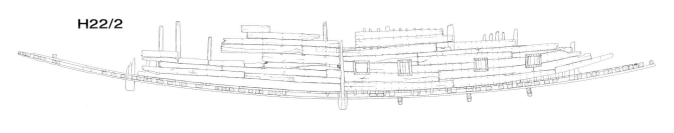

H23

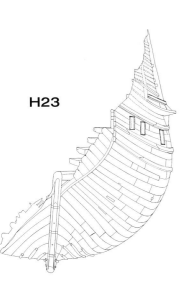

H24/1

H24/2

PICTURE CREDITS

ACKNOWLEDGEMENTS

The illustrations in this book have either been drawn by the author based on examples from the *Mary Rose* or are the author's own reconstruction drawings. Where drawings have been taken from *Mary Rose* examples, then the archaeological drawings have been reconstructed to show how the originals would have been; for example, crushed items have been redrawn to their original shapes, bent spoons straightened, or the missing half of the compass case drawn in along with the string used to tie it together. All photographs are from the author's collection unless otherwise stated here.

The drawings that are the copyright of and reproduced by permission of the Mary Rose Trust are those in Chapter 12, except the section drawings and roman numerals. Also reproduced by permission of the Mary Rose Trust are the images of the author underwater (Fig 104) and of the *Mary Rose* being raised (Fig 103), both taken by Christopher Dobbs.

The front cover image of the Anthony Roll and figures 1, 5, 18 and 24 are reproduced by permission of the Pepys Library, Magdalene College, Cambridge.

The photograph of the museum on the back cover flap was reproduced by kind permission of MindWorks Marketing.

Fig 91 on page 56 is © The British Library Board (Cotton Augustus I.i, f. 18).

I am indebted to the Mary Rose Trust in particular the chief executives Martyn Heighton, Charles Payton and John Lippiet for employing and supporting me while I finished off the recording of the ship. For general and intellectual support at the Trust, I thank my colleagues; the late Andy Elkerton, Alexzandra Hildred, Christopher Dobbs and Maurice Young. For support with illustrations, especially the ordnance, I thank RA Anderson Smith. No publication of mine could be done without the long-suffering but freely given emotional support of my parents and partner Tor. No writer can be without their publisher, initially John Lee whose concept it was, however any factual mistakes or omissions are mine.